One Mother's Story
Raising Deaf Children:
An Educator Becomes A Parent

By Barbara Luetke-Stahlman, Ph.D.

Published by
Modern
Signs Press, Inc.

International Standard Book Number 0-916708-27-6
Library of Congress Catalog Number 96-76281

Publisher

Modern Signs Press, Incorporated
P.O. Box 1181
Los Alamitos, CA 90720
310/596-8548, 310/493-4168 V/TDD
FAX 310/795-6614

Cover Design by Diane Schmidt

First Printing, 1996

Printed in the United States of America

DEDICATION

One Mother's Story is dedicated to the following
mothers:

Bette Walgran Luetke, who birthed Barbara,
Rita Stahlman Meinert, who birthed Kent,
Pam Fite, who found us Mary Pat,
Linda Pittman, who gave us Marcy,
Judy Conley and Celia Harris, who typed this book, and
Esther Zawolkow and Gerilee Gustason, who
edited and published it.

Foreword

All of us in the field of education of deaf and hard of hearing children, or in the field of preparing teachers for these youth, are expected to know 'the' answers when working with parents and teachers. Not only are we expected to know 'the' most appropriate way to teach these youth, but we are expected to be able to analyze and comment upon the many issues in the field today: placement options, communication modalities, languages and systems, amplification, Deaf culture, cochlear implants.   Yet these issues are far from simple, and choices and answers always child-dependent. We speak of focusing on the child. It is easy to forget that young children, while they have minds and wills and personalities of their own, are still children---and parents have the right and the responsibility of making many choices that impact upon their children.

Being a professional in the field does mean we may come to the task of parenting with more information than many parents do. But it does not mean the choices are any simpler or easier.   Dr. Barbara Luetke-Stahlman and her husband, Kent, already had two hearing daughters when they adopted a deaf girl of 2-1/2, and later a second daughter of 4. They already had some experience as parents. Yet, as you will see from the following story, the emotional turmoil and difficulty of making choices still existed for them.

There are many things in Barbara's story to which I can relate. I, too, have been a professional in the field of education of deaf youth for many years. I, too, chose to adopt a deaf daughter a few years ago. She, like Barbara's, came from a disadvantaged background.   She, too, has had a cochlear implant---at her own request. But she has not used it as well as have Barbara's girls. Her experience, and the family which she and I now make, are different from Barbara's and her family. Yet I too have experienced the 'dislocation' of sitting on the other side of the table during IEP staffings. I too have sought ways to give this child every advantage, while making sure she has an identity as a deaf child. I have gained some insights and ideas from Barbara's story,. Perhaps the most telling identification with her experience has come when she describes the reaction of some deaf individuals (Deaf individuals?) to her decision to use SEE and to get cochlear implants for the girls. We are professionals. We do not go into things blindly. Yet we have both been vilified for our decisions. Do we love our girls? You bet! Do we deny their deafness? By no means. Do we love them <u>because</u> they are deaf? No, but because they are who they are. I do not love my daughter for her ears or her blue eyes. I love her because she is Ashlee, just as Barbara loves all four of her daughters for who they are.

Parental choices and decisions are complex and difficult. Parents do not need emotional blackmail or criticism or coercion. They need clear, impartial information and they need emotional support. It is our hope that Barbara's story will help other parents understand that we all share many of the same experiences and emotions, and help both professionals and deaf adults understand a little better what these experiences and emotions can be like for some of us.

Gerilee Gustason

ONE MOTHER'S STORY
RAISING DEAF CHILDREN: AN EDUCATOR BECOMES A PARENT
by
Barbara Luetke-Stahlman, Ph.D.

Prologue

Sometimes, depending on when I go to bed the night before or what is cycling through my mind, I awaken before Kent's alarm goes off at five a.m.. This is my preference: I know from experience that I will wake him if I get up, and so I have come to enjoy the feeling of being held a prisoner in our bed. It gives me time to plan my morning, thinking in detail about one of the children or my work--or listen to the comforting sound of Kent's breathing. On other days, I awaken, amazed to find he is already in the shower. How did I sleep through that obnoxious alarm, I wonder. Long ago, we made a pact that he would always say good-bye before he hurried off to teach in Kansas City, Missouri. It is a 45-minute drive in traffic from the southern suburb of Olathe where we live. Most days, Kent can't wait to get there!

For the next half hour or so, I bask in what is usually the only time I have alone all day. It is mine. I read, eat my Cheerios, take the first shower (well, it's technically the second, counting Kent's), and often straighten the living room or start a load of wash. It is the quiet before the storm.

Either Lori, our live-in college student, or Breeze, our daughter, gets into the shower next. Usually, it's Lori. She is a bright, charming, deaf woman with whom we have traded room and board for child care for the semester. We are surprised at how well it has all worked.

Breeze, our hearing, 14 year old daughter, has an amazing schedule. She is a top student and involved in orchestra, choir, basketball, the fall play, and a myriad of social activities. If she has to be at school early, she snaps out of bed with a self-determination and drive equal to that of her father's; if not, I have to remember to call to her by 6:30. Among the three of us blow-drying our hair and getting ready for school or work, we trip the fuse marked "bathroom" almost every morning.

Marcy and Mary Pat are like clocks, wandering in to find me by 6:40. I love the way they'll stagger in, looking for a snuggle or a pat. If they start by arguing about what I have laid out on their floor the night before for them to wear to school, I just turn away. I have been trying for years to convince my girls that I need a slow starting morning and a solo shower. They go dress independently and I don't see them again for ten minutes. There is an order: clothes on, pajamas put away, bed made, socks and shoes on, hair combed, equipment on-- THEN they can come back and talk with me again. They are now independent about dressing, but we have worked long and hard at it. Mary Pat is six; Marcy four. They share a room and most of their clothes. They are both bright, creative, and deaf.

Hannah is always the last up, the last dressed, and the longest in the bathroom. Almost routinely, I will go in, hug her awake, say the same commands that work with the others, and her response will be to roll over and catch a few more minutes of rest. "Hurry up," I call to her as I leave her room, peek at the little girls, make a mental note of Breeze's progress, and head for my room to finish dressing, putting on make-up, or, on a good morning, writing the final notes of a project laying on my desk. Hannah, nine and hearing, always catches up by the time we are heading out the door.

Either Lori helps downstairs with breakfast, or the kids are on their own. If Breeze is ahead of schedule, she is wonderful about reaching for the needed foods, supervising the microwave and toaster, or turning arguments into conversations. I stay upstairs, helping Marcy get her harness and cochlear implant on, and getting her started on a computer program that facilitates auditory training. Twenty minutes later, I usually have myself ready, our bed made, and my book bag repacked. I check on Marcy and send her down for breakfast. By that time, Mary Pat is usually finished with her breakfast and she comes up to work on the audition program.

Three days a week I take Breeze over to the junior high about 7:30. Usually we pick up two of her friends, too. In some small way I feel this might put me ahead with these families, should Breeze need a ride home later in the day. Two years ago, when she called from school at noon and said that if she didn't get a physical THAT DAY, she wouldn't be able to try out for basketball, it was one such neighbor who drove her. I remain eternally impressed by such generosity. Another plus about these mornings is that, although I have to sit in traffic, I do get to school earlier than usual and can find a parking place. On Tuesday and Thursday I have to park about a mile away and try to convince myself that the walk is good for my health.

In between what appears a sensible, orderly progression of morning activities, either Lori or I make lunches. It is also my responsibility to go through the book bags, writing notes back to teachers, working on Marcy's speech or language, compiling show-and-tell or objects needed for units (e.g., could you send a dinosaur to school today?), and loading the dishwasher. On the days Lori has to leave early and I drive the little girls to school, the kitchen is left half strewn with toys, silverware, books, and notes. Yet, most days Hannah and

Mary Pat get a fair amount of reading done between breakfast and departure; the television is not allowed on.

Probably once a week, I don't even attempt to get to work with the other rush hour commuters and instead spend a few minutes straightening this or that, finding "must haves" for school, talking with the children about projects and events--well, you know, being a mom. Before Lori, there was almost always screaming in the morning, less quality time conversing, worse lunches, and many lost library books. I almost never had time for make-up, although I used to joke that at least my clothes were always clean. When people would ask me how I did "it," I would promptly reply, "not very well." These days, I have the same recurring thought as I drive up to Kansas City to the KU Medical Center: "I love my family; I love my work. I wish I could balance all our needs better."

Kent and I work, the kids go to school. When Marcy, our preschooler, only has a half day, she goes to the home of a deaf friend for child care. Kent and/or Lori are home by the time the girls start arriving. I don't think much about them except when it rains or snows: will someone take Marcy's equipment off and zip her coat? Will Hannah and Mary Pat wear their boots home or just splash along in their tennis shoes? Will Kent or Lori think to pick them up so they don't have to walk? Remember there is hot chocolate in the kitchen cupboard...

Except on the night I teach, I leave work about 5:00 and go work out. By 6:00 I am running errands as I wind my way home. Kent takes university classes a couple of nights each week and Breeze often has sports or music related events in the late afternoon or evening. We have tried to get the kids to follow a regular schedule of activities as soon as they walk in: hang up coats, put their back packs in the kitchen for me to check later, eat a snack, Lori to work with Marcy or read to

Mary Pat, everyone help fix dinner and clean up, no television until 7:00, etc. At least one night a week, the little girls go to the school for the deaf and stay through dinner. Everyone usually spends time on the computer and Hannah and Breeze each practice violin for 35-45 minutes a day. If Kent is home, he will rotate from girl to girl, helping with homework, supervising practicing, talking about school needs, etc. About once a month he will take one girl and do something special with just her (out for pizza, along to run his errands, out to get something needed for school). He or Lori cook all the dinners.

Having had time to think and plan as I drive home, I usually arrive with a specific agenda. I will spend some time talking to the little girls, solving someone's problems, talk to parents of deaf children on the phone, or do laundry. As soon as the little ones are in bed, I try to talk to Hannah, then Breeze, then, having spent the day with people and on the telephone, I usually head upstairs for the quiet of my bedroom to read. I save professional reading for this time of day--it doesn't take long though and my eyes get heavy; I always sleep soundly through the night. Kent, having studied down in his office basement for a couple of hours, usually joins me about ten o'clock.

And then it starts again. By the time the weekend comes, we are ready to crawl into the cocoon of our family life and do little. The older girls have violin lessons on Saturday mornings and Breeze needs to be taken to Kansas City Youth Symphony rehearsals on Sunday afternoons. Usually most of us will make it to Quaker meeting on Sunday morning and Kent and I stop to work out together about half of those Sundays as we head back to Olathe. We do little entertaining, avoid fast-food restaurants, and discourage the girls from complicated, involved plans. There is, however, lots of napping, cleaning, television watching, reading, and desk work--done at a slow pace with lots of interruptions. Kent and

I usually take our dog, Patch, for at least one long, hour walk. The kids either invite friends to sleep over or spend long hours with other families. If it is not raining or snowing, Mary Pat and Marcy swing or play house endlessly in the backyard.

The Beginning

The decision to adopt a deaf child had roots back to my childhood. A little deaf boy that came occasionally to visit our neighbors, a deaf shoe repairman whose shop was near my Dad's office, a deaf cousin who danced across the lawn of her lake home like a fairy with a white harness...

Later, coming of age in Madison, Wisconsin, I studied "behavioral disabilities" (special education), participated in the Women's Movement, demonstrated against the War (in Vietnam), and became a supporter of gay rights. Aware that I was a person of white middle class privilege I felt I needed to do more than live a productive life. I wanted to give something back to my country, my world.

When Kent and I married, we agreed that we would birth two children of our own and then adopt a deaf child. Breeze Elizabeth was born in 1978 and Hannah Schell in 1983. A month after Hannah's birth, we filled out our first forms and had our first interview for adoption. Five years and many forms and interviews later, we were still waiting. The social referral system did not seem to work for us. We were registered with national networking systems of special needs adoption and we completed courses and the necessary forms with local agencies. We were persistent and well-educated, and yet we saw children slip by us. We could not afford foreign adoption, so we continued to subscribe to adoption journals and newsletters, talk to contacts, and raise our birth children. For the first ten years of our marriage, our plan to adopt a deaf child did not seem as if it would ever be realized.

Some Background

I had spent four months at a school for the deaf in Tijuana in 1973, returned to the University of Wisconsin to complete my undergraduate degree with my class and with honors. Then I worked a year as a teacher's aide with deaf children who had cognitive impairments at Badger School in Madison as I awaited acceptance to graduate school. I jumped for joy around my small one room apartment the day Don Moores called to offer me stipend support in his program at the University of Minnesota, and left four years of organizing with the United Farm Workers to study with him. I became a certified teacher of the deaf in 1975.

In the years that followed, I taught for five years, got married, had a baby (Breeze), followed Don Moores to Pennsylvania State University for a doctorate (studying both deaf education and bilingual education), and became a professor. Kent, a computer wizard and secondary math teacher, relocated repeatedly so that I could further my career. We had another child (Hannah) while I was at the University of Nebraska-Omaha and moved shortly afterwards to Sycamore, Illinois. I became the director of the Deaf Education program, wrote a text that included strategies and methods for teaching deaf and hard-of-hearing children with my colleague, John Luckner, and became more serious about finding and adding another child to our family.

Unable to find a child to adopt, Kent and I worked for about a year to bear another child ourselves. We drove down to Chicago monthly, did all the things we had heard others talk about as they attempted to conceive, and eventually decided we did not have the time, energy, or interest in continuing these efforts. I sent another batch of announcements to magazines and newspapers that focused on deafness, stating our desire to adopt, and I continued to publish articles related to my field in nationally circulated publications.

When Pam Fite, a lead teacher in northern Texas, called me to tell me about the availability of a deaf child in her program, Breeze was nine and Hannah was four. Pam had read one of my announcements in a magazine called "The Voice" and had also read a publication I had written for "Perspectives" magazine. Pam had already watched as one deaf child in her program was adopted by a family who was uninvolved in learning to sign and didn't participate to a large extent in educational goals. She was determined that this second adoptable child would be placed with a family that would communicate and advocate for her. Luckily, we already had had a home study completed and were registered as foster parents in our community. We sent our papers to the Texas social worker and waited. And we tried to become accustomed to the realization that after so many years of talking about our plans to adopt, we were actually being considered as a child's parents.

We heard later that over 200 families applied to adopt the child who was then called "Annie." Because of Pam's insistence that the little girl needed a family that could communicate immediately with her in sign and the responsiveness of the social worker who handled our case, Annie came to live with us in August, 1988 when she was 2 1/2 years old. I wanted to give her a name that would be both easy to speechread and easy to pronounce. We decided on Mary Pat, after Mary Pat Moeller, an outstanding professional at Boys Town National Research Hospital who had helped hundreds of families with children who were deaf or hard-of-hearing.

Mary Pattie, her social worker, and her foster mom, Char, arrived in Chicago on the Saturday the weekend before Hannah was to start kindergarten. Odd as it seems now, we weren't completely sure even at that point, that she soon was going to be ours. No one had ever explained the adoption process to us, or what the various steps meant. We accepted whatever the social worker said and waited for the next bit of information. For this reason, it was at least a year before we felt safe in expressing our disappointment at the timing of Mary Pat's placement. We were teachers; we did not work during the summer. And yet, because the social worker had five weeks of vacation due her and wanted to bring Mary Pat to us, we had to wait for our daughter until August. We could have used that summer time to bond as a family. But, most importantly, Hannah would not have had to share her entry into school with a new sibling, who stole the limelight.

We continued to feel insecure in those first few days and weeks. I distinctly remember laying with Kent after we had put Mary Pat to bed for her first night with us. Hannah tells me now that Mary Pat cried a lot and I was stern with her. I don't remember that part. I do remember holding Kent's hand under the blankets, and us admitting to each other how scared we were with the thought of having this new daughter. We had birthed two children. We had had several years to plan and dream about raising them...and then that specific nine months to feel each infant growing, preparing for birth inside me. It had been eight short months since I had first gotten the call from Texas about Mary Pat, a deaf preschooler, who needed a good home. Now, here she was! With hearing aids, a suitcase of clothes, a few toys, potty trained, able to feed herself, and, yes, it appeared she was going to sleep through the night! She was far from being a helpless infant. She was an active two and a half-year old with a determined personality.

We knew we could provide a good home for Mary Pat, a good family experience, a good life. But we lay there, holding hands in the dark of the night, wondering about schooling and signing, about our hearing girls' needs, and about all the things of which we weren't very confident. It was an awesome night, filled with a heavy feeling of responsibility. It is etched forever in my mind.

We had our first staffing to enroll Mary Pat in school three days after her arrival. It was a small group of professionals, Kent, and me. Everyone was excited and happy for us. Mary Pat was placed on Tuesday through Friday mornings in the Early Childhood classroom in our neighborhood school. She was the only deaf child.

We were thankful that Mary Pat was to be enrolled in a half-day diagnostic educational placement, but we also felt a need to augment her education at home. Perhaps because of my deaf education background, I knew what would need to be accomplished if she were going to be able to handle regular kindergarten and attend public school with Hannah. We had three years to get ready. She was almost three years old and knew but ten signs.

Early Work in the Home With Mary Pattie

Both Kent and I worked outside the home, so we looked for ways within our home activities that we could incorporate speech, audition and language work for Mary Pattie in home routines. It wasn't our style to sit down in tutorial sessions with her.

We believed that to survive and access the hearing society, Mary Pat would need to be able to use whatever speech she could develop to augment her signing of English. Mary Pat had been fitted with hearing aids several months before she came to live with us and so we tried to facilitate her audition (listening) skills at the same time that we worked with her speech articulation and speech reading skills. We tried to pair stimulating sounds to movements that were part of our daily routines. Mary Pat seemed to enjoy this simple addition of sounds to accompany common actions. For example, when we lifted her up we would increase the pitch of our voice as we said the word, "U-U-U-U-U-U-P". We would swing her around for a quick airplane twirl on the way to the highchair and make an airplane sound as we went. Often she would request this ride and make a similar sound. Sometimes when she was in our arms turning to watch something of interest we would make a sound that was associated with what she was seeing. It didn't take any extra time to accompany movements with sound and it seemed to be stimulating the little residual hearing that Mary Pat had. We would discuss these activities as a family and thoughtfully suggest additional speech, audition, and English language opportunities that might be available in our home routines.

We also took Mary Pattie to a speech clinic at the University. This was because the speech pathologist who worked at the early childhood program was just learning to sign, and Mary Pat didn't have the language to understand much of what she wanted her to do. The clinic was located about 15 minutes from our home, and we went there once or twice a week. We'd park the car and then carry Mary Pat because it was a long walk for her tiny legs. We would often talk to her on this walk. Even though her head might be turned away from us, we said simple phrases like "Look, it's Brandon." Even at her young age Mary Pat seemed to realize that because our hands were occupied with holding her, we couldn't sign and our speech-only was necessary under these circumstances. We would just use simple words like "look" or "there" and say "yes" to acknowledge her pointing. We were not sure if she understood all the words at first, but we would repeat them in these common routines, sign them when our hands were free, and, over a period of time, she began to speech read some of our spoken language.

We also began trying to pair sounds that we were teaching to Mary Pat with meaningful words that she already knew in sign. For example, we taught her that a cow said "moo," and a ghost said "boo," and Santa said "Ho, Ho, Ho," and we encouraged her to say "bye, bye" whenever it was appropriate and "uh-huh" in a positive response to request since she couldn't produce the word "yes." We also bought or borrowed toys and dolls that produced sounds she could partially hear and to which she could respond.

We were the type of family that spent endless hours in the car running errands and taxiing children to a variety of activities. We tried to make use of this time in the driver's seat by working on audition, speech, and English language skills with our child. She was at the detection stage of listening, trying to consistently indicate whether sound was present or not. We would turn the car radio on and off and try to have her tell us if she could hear music or not. If music was playing, we would have her clap or sway to its rhythm. When the radio was off we would provide the language that normally would accompany that situation. For example, we might say "I don't hear anything." We did this frequently as we ran errands and Mary Pat would imitate our responses to the few environmental sounds she could hear.

We also sang and signed many nursery rhymes to our daughter. We tried to pick those that included contemporary English and for which some meaning could be explained. I had read that an understanding of rhymes was important in learning to read proficiently so we sang or said these nursery rhymes whenever we found ourselves waiting in a doctor's office or sitting together at some quiet moment. She learned Twinkle, Twinkle, Little Star, Mary Had a Little Lamb, Three Men in A Tub, Little Boy Blue, and so on. We played games like "Patty Cake" using different pitches and volumes although it seemed that Mary Pat had no awareness of high and low sounds.

Some people have asked us over the years why we used signs at all with Mary Pat, but our daughter clearly needed signs. She had so much to communicate and her speech was very unintelligible.

Our Signing

Every family member had been learning to speak and sign simultaneously to Mary Pat to the best of our ability since she had arrived. Our hearing girls did not seem to understand that some words in conceptual sign might have several signs for the same word. One day Hannah, who was five years old at the time, asked me how to sign RUN. I started to explain that it depended on what you were saying. I gave her several examples. In the middle of what seemed to me to be a very appropriate explanation, Hannah interrupted, "Mom," she asked innocently, "What's the sign for run?" That was the day we adopted the philosophy of using one word, one sign --- no matter what the meaning. Signing in English seemed easier for a family whose home language was English.

It was easiest for our family to sign the words exactly as they were written or spoken. For example, we signed all the figurative language that appeared in children's books. If the expression "runny nose" or the expression "neat as a pin" appeared on the page, we would sign the exact English for these words. This method of communication allowed not only Kent and me as parents, but Breeze and Hannah also, to communicate and read to Mary Pat in our family's language.

We also put a children's vocabulary book (of the Richard Scary genre) in a recipe book holder on the kitchen table near Mary Pat's chair. Each day we would try to read one page of this book with her and discuss the new vocabulary. We would challenge ourselves to look up the signs we needed to carry on conversations about these pages. For example, at breakfast, Breeze might have signed "can you find the toast" or "I see the toaster, do you? or "where is our shiny toaster?" We kept this practice up for at least a year and all learned lots of signs in this way.

Signing and Reading

As educators we valued reading and our home was filled with books. We knew that reading to young children was necessary for promoting later literacy so we made an effort not to leave Mary Pat out of the literacy activities that our hearing children had experienced at her age. We used a plastic cookbook stand to hold the books, or tied alligator clips to a string and looped it around our neck so that pages could be held open while we signed. Other times we would use our knees or her hands to hold the book so that our hands were free for signing.

Signing even stories written for preschoolers is a challenge! Sometimes we followed our child's lead and named the pictures in the books as we turned the pages. Yet on other occasions, we read the actual words of the story. This meant we had to look up a lot of words in our sign dictionary and fingerspell words for which there were no signs. However, we thought both types of reading activities were important and that motivated us to not just point and label pictures at every reading session. We knew that like all children, Mary Pat loved to hear the same story over and over so we would challenge ourselves to learn the signs to a particular story and read that to her until she seemed to tire of it. This gave us lots of practice with the signing of words and affixes that we did not typically use in our daily conversation. Eventually, upon reading the story for about the tenth time, we had to look up fewer words. The fingerspelling of short words (under five letters) seemed very acceptable to Mary Pat and she began to spell all or part of a dozen words just from this type of exposure.

We also carried a small shoebox of little books in the car so we could use car time to look at small age-appropriate books. If Mary Pat was sitting in the front seat, she often initiated a conversation about something that she saw in a book. Kent and I found that we could acknowledge and label pictures while still driving, although I received several speeding tickets. Friends later joked that the reason I eventually had to leave the state was to get a fresh start on my driving record.

Environmental Print and Language

Running errands with our older children had taught us that children typically labeled stores and signs that they passed frequently. So for Mary Pat, we took photographs of restaurants, stores, the library, and other local businesses, and we practiced labeling these at home. Usually this type of drill was done for just a few minutes before a meal and a stack of materials sat waiting in a corner of the kitchen counter.

We also sometimes taped cards on the dashboard if we were going to a particular location so that Mary Pat could begin to match up and make sense of the pictures. Sometimes we chose some signs to label these destinations from our sign book. For example, the EAGLE FOOD STORE or the CORNER MARKET. Other stores like K-Mart, we fingerspelled. We invented some signs for some stores and locations. For example: Wendy's and Hardee's we signed like RESTAURANT and letter cued (signing Wendy's with W's instead of Rs). We also asked deaf adults and other parents of deaf children in our community about their signs for stores and locations We found that although most of these words were fingerspelled there were some local signs that were useful to us as we matched labels and logos to our spoken communication in signs. Mary Pat began to comment on landmarks in route to our destinations.

Symbolic Play

Knowing that play was an important link to language, we gave Mary Pat many opportunities to use symbolic, representational play. For example, she would use a wooden spoon as a trumpet or a mixer while "helping" me in the kitchen. When Mary Pat was pretending to mix something in the kitchen, we would ask her what she was making, who was coming for dinner, or who might be expected to clean up afterwards. If we received no reply, we would suggest real or imaginary answers to these questions.

I have always thought that it was fortunate that Mary Pat could play at home with Hannah and converse in sign and that we saw this behavior daily. It was amazing to me the number of professionals who commented during her preschool and kindergarten years that she could only engage in parallel play with her peers and preferred to interact with her interpreters rather than the hearing children. We would report the symbolic play episodes that went on for hours in our home, and remind our team members that advanced play necessitates a shared communication system. The need wasn't with Mary Pat's play skills, it was with the inability of her hearing peers to sign. What seemed a preference to play with interpreters instead of children, could be explained in terms of who was able to have a complex conversation with her.

Learning To Sign

Everybody in our family had been learning sign informally since Mary Pat's arrival. We found that practice became easier when it was mingled with typical family routines such as dressing, eating, toilet-training, and going out and coming home. These activities provided excellent opportunities to label ideas, practice vocabulary, ask questions, and simply converse. We chose language to practice in sign that we would use naturally in these situations. For example, we would sign and say something like "Wow, there's a lot of pencils here" and not, "Look, look, many, many pencils." If I wanted something I would say, "Give it to me," not "Give it to mother." In those situations where I called myself "mom," I would sign "mom" and not "mother." We tried to provide authentic, genuine English in sign and speech to our daughter. Mary Pat brought "family time" to a busy household!

We included whoever was available and sat in a semicircle to do puzzles, matching games, art projects or chores together, signing and talking. Mary Pat was practicing English and the rest of us were practicing sign. If a family member couldn't be with us one time, we accepted it and tried to arrange the next session at a time when they could join us. We also reinforced any family member for looking up signs in the sign dictionary that we used. Such a resource was vital to our sign development. We kept several of these books in various locations throughout our house and in our car. We also thought that looking up signs set a good example for Mary Pat who used this dictionary by herself as she got older to look up unknown words she encountered while reading.

Members of our family also began to lead or attend formal sign classes in our community. Kent and Breeze, then

10 years old, audited a college level sign class taught by a deaf adult, Guy Vollmar. Hannah, our five year old, went to a children's sign class that was offered by the local park service on Saturdays.

We also helped start a children's sign program in our neighborhood school. As part of a pilot program, the park service hired a teacher-in-training from the university deaf education program to teach two sign classes at our neighborhood school. One was for K-2nd grade and one for 3rd-5th grade during the students' recess period once a week. Three students from each class in the school attended the sign classes. The students then taught the other children in their room the signs that they learned after they said the pledge to the flag each morning. Some teachers made bulletin boards of the sign pages that came back with the children from the classes. Others made booklets. About 300 children learned some basic signs through this program and we benefited from the results when Mary Pat was out in the community and children could sign to her.

When our deaf friend, Mark, joined our local swim team along with Breeze and Hannah, we made a family project out of compiling a sign booklet for the members of the team. The booklet began with 40 sentences that we heard often at swim practice and swim meets and included the names of the team members as well as some basic rules about signing. The rest of the book was pages xeroxed out of sign books that included the signs needed for the sentences. Members of the team passed this book up and down the benches while they waited for their events, learning to sign functional things to Mark: "Get out of my lane;" "Did you leave your towel in the locker room?" "Win your heat!"

A Disabled Family?

Our family was very focused on Mary Pat and how to accommodate her communication needs within our home. Time went by in a rush. Sadly, I hardly remember anything about Hannah's kindergarten year. I do remember that at some point we were forced to pay attention to our middle child. She had been complaining for weeks about being tired, but we had chosen to ignore her and sent her off to school. She was diagnosed as having CMV, a virus that affected her very much like mononucleosis affects a teenager. When it was obvious that she was sick, we felt extremely guilty, realizing that we had been too absorbed in Mary Pat's needs. Our life had revolved around finding a signing babysitter, IEP staffings, training an interpreter for the daycare center, and establishing and attending parents meetings,.

We began to focus on becoming a less disabled family; to normalize our routines. Kent and I began exercising regularly again and paying closer attention to our hearing children. I would like to believe that our older girls were more sensitive, more giving, and more understanding of special needs because of their parents' decision to adopt. Yet, they had little control and certainly could not have predicted the specific effects that the decision had on their lives. It is a burden that Kent and I will always bear. I wondered if somewhere down the road, there might be animosity about the sharing that they did, and I began to read adoption materials in preparation for it. We started taking each girl out for dinner alone once a week and telling them often how special we thought they were.

Out of Control At the IEP Meetings: A New Experience

Mary Pat's official IEP meeting was slated for December. It was at this meeting that the decision would be made as to how she would be educated for the spring semester. We knew that in the past all deaf children had been sent to the cooperative program an hour away from our home in Rockford. However, we felt Mary Pat's adoptive status presented special needs, and therefore, special programming. We slept restlessly realizing that things had changed since our first meeting. Then, everyone had been so excited, laughing about my role as a professor in deaf education and parent advocate and how it had changed: I had moved around to the other side of the table.

Other parents shared with us that they felt that because I was a professor in deaf education, I should have insight into the process of these staffings. Then and now they confided in us that they are sure that my occupation influences the opportunities and options that are offered us. True or not, in the early days, such parental opinions only added to my guilt. I felt unprepared and ineffective at the staffings. I worried endlessly about the issues involving Mary Pat's education that faced our family and tried to learn the skills to advocate effectively for her. Kent and I would discuss strategies to use in the meetings, only to walk out of them feeling unheard and helpless. It all quickly became "we" versus "them".

I think the basic issue in Illinois was one of control. We would discuss often why we were having so much trouble having our values heard by the educators on the team. It wasn't money, it wasn't Mary Pat's needs, it was simply that the administrators did not want us to think that we could influence where or for how long during the day our daughter attended school.

What I had known previously about staffings as a professor clashed with the reality of our experiences. Perhaps it was only that I came down from the ivory tower of academia. However, it certainly seemed that assumptions had been made about where Mary Pat would go to school and for how long each day she would be educated long before we actually attended the meeting. The team process, including us as part of the team, seemed to have been side-stepped.

The administrators at our staffing told us that Mary Pat could only be educated for half the day if she attended the early childhood program in which she was currently enrolled, but full-day if she traveled by bus to the cooperative program in Rockford. Yet, if our child had been hearing, she would have spent the day in a local daycare center until I picked her up in late afternoon. We did not understand why she couldn't be placed in this normalized placement. She was a normal child; simply deaf. Members of the team looked in dismay at us; we looked in dismay at them.

Perhaps if we hadn't already successfully raised two children, we would have more readily accepted the school staff's professional decisions about placement, sign choice, socialization, etc. But, fortunately or unfortunately, that was not the case. We were middle class, college-educated people. It seemed very logical to us a newly-adopted deaf child should not be bused away from home. It shocked us to have to discuss basic decisions that effected our family with so many people at a meeting. And, despite our requests to involve the school social worker, who we thought might provide support, no one would discuss adoption needs at these meetings.

Although we thought Mary Pat would benefit from a full-day program, we worked with our team to eventually decide that she would continue to attend the half-day early childhood program in our home school. Her days, starting in January, were a crazy quilt of placements!

The public school early childhood program did not hold preschool on Mondays so that the staff could do home visits. (However, in the two years that Mary Pat was in the program, we never had one home visit!) On Mondays, then, she attended a day care center near my work. We paid for the interpreter that facilitated the communication between the teachers, hearing children and her.

For the mornings during the rest of the week, she attended the early childhood program in our home school. She was the only deaf child and the school provided an interpreter. Most of the children in her class had cognitive delays or speech and language problems. The children with communication needs did not initiate conversation much at all. No child ever attempted to talk with our daughter. We observed about once every two weeks that spring and became concerned that Mary Pat had no one to play with and no one from whom to learn language other than the adults in the classroom. School was over at noon, and Mary Pat was bused to the home of a woman in the community who signed. There she ate, napped, and played with the sitter's hearing children until Kent could fetch her about 4:00. We hoped that at our staffing for the next school year we could persuade the school personnel to provide one consistent integrated placement for her each day of the week. No other three year old, we argued, had to move through so many environments.

Twenty-one people attended our spring meeting. Votes were taken on various issues, although we as parents were never allowed to vote and would have been extremely out-numbered had we been. I remember one supervisor saying to me as we stood outside the old administration building in our little rural town, "We only want what is best for your daughter." But how can so many people know what is best? I sincerely wondered. We had not been asked to sign either the

January or May IEP. We didn't realize until we moved to a Kansas school district how odd this was.

Deaf Way

When school was out that summer, we needed a break. We packed our bags and headed for Washington, D.C. and Gallaudet University to attend an international event, Deaf Way. I had been told on the telephone that this was an event that would make us proud to have a deaf family member. This certainly was the case. While our children participated i n a fabulous daycare program, visiting the sites of Washington, D.C., mingling with deaf adults, and learning to sign more proficiently, Kent and I attended workshops and seminars, socialized with deaf adults and hearing professionals, and learned a great deal about deafness.

When we first arrived at Deaf Way, we had been "closet signers," thinking our English signing would be ridiculed. But day after day deaf and hearing adults would join our family as we picnicked on the Gallaudet football field and applauded our ability to communicate with Mary Pat. We felt so rewarded and relieved. We had had a good vacation, and we were proud of the positive changes that our family was making to promote the growth of our deaf daughter.

Fall, 1989

Despite our hopes, Mary Pat began the fall with a confusing schedule. She received OT, PT, and some deaf education services at the daycare on Monday and remained enrolled in the early education program Tuesday through Friday mornings. After several attempts to find socialization activities for her in the afternoon, the school district placed her in two different programs in our community: One met on

Tuesday and Thursday and the other on Wednesday and Friday. She sometimes attended a program at the nearby high school as part of her morning program that was taught by high school students. There were different groups of hearing children at all these sites. The deaf educator, hired that fall to serve Mary Pat and another deaf preschooler, functioned as the interpreter in the high school program when she was not out in the hall disciplining the younger deaf boy.

Kent and I were not at all happy with all the changing. Our daughter was in four different classes a week, being served by eight different teachers, and co-existing with 45 different children! There seemed to be no coordination among the professionals involved in these programs and the lack of consistency in signing slowed the acquisition of language. After unsuccessful attempts to streamline the program into one or two placements, we filed for due process that October. That Valentine's Day was a depressing one for me as I helped my daughter sign her name to 45 valentines. No one in her school programs seemed to have any awareness of the stress that Mary Pat endured as she traveled to these various classes. She began wetting her pants, standing by our front door each morning asking where she would "go first, and then second."

Going To Due Process

In the fall of 1989, we hired a lawyer who was a parent of a special needs child and who had reviewed our materials. She thought we should easily win our case. Mary Pat had been evaluated for full-day placement by a psychologist who could not sign and therefore, could not communicate with her. She could not interact with the children in her programs. Two afternoons a week her teacher of the deaf never saw her and had only visited her at her nursery school placement once. She was being bounced all over town in the course of a week.

We made the long drive to Chicago several times to talk with the lawyer. As expensive as she was, we felt this financial commitment was necessary if we were to have our daughter placed in an appropriate setting. Personally, I could not bear the pressure of knowing whether the decisions I was making were correct and felt I needed legal guidance as we worked through the due process system.

On the day of our due process, Sharon Freagon, a colleague from my university department, and one set of faithful parents of a deaf child joined us for the grueling twelve hour hearing. Memories of that day come back to me at the oddest times. It was an experience I would wish for no one. The money that the school spent arguing our case could have paid for <u>two</u> teachers of the deaf the following year. By the end of the day, the due process officer was exhausted and inattentive. The pregnant stenographer asked for breaks repeatedly.

We lost at level one and went on to level two. We lost again, and decided to move. We sold our house, paid $8,000 in lawyer fees, and went on vacation. Our older girls were tired of conversations about Mary Pat, the due process, and the stress that the whole situation had caused. After being hoarse for a year, my voice returned as we hiked and rafted with Uncle Bill in the Montana mountains.

Moving

Positions were available at both Gallaudet University and the University of Kansas to direct Deaf Education programs. I preferred Kansas City and called directors of the school programs in the surrounding suburbs with regard to the education of children who were deaf or hard of hearing. I hoped to choose a program that would allow us access to an experience that hearing children took for granted: attendance for Mary Pat at our home school .

We bought a home three blocks from a neighborhood school that enrolled a dozen deaf students. Mary Pat would not be bused and could walk with Hannah to school. We were also influenced by the large number of deaf adults that lived in Olathe, our new community.

On the day that our family moved to Kansas, I took the girls to the local pool. It seemed to me that I had not been there for more than five minutes when three different people approached me. They must have seen us signing. Two were hearing teachers of the deaf and one was a deaf adult. This seemed like heaven to me. We had been told that there were 10,000 deaf people in the greater Kansas City area; we had probably left a total of ten deaf children and adults in our town in Illinois. The new friends began to tell me about all the activities and resources involving deafness in our new community. Within the next few weeks, we had a vibrating fire alarm installed on Mary Pat's bed by the fire department and a man come to our home to help us hook up our lights and captioner. The school for the deaf put us on a mailing list for the parent newsletter and let us know about upcoming activities that involved deaf people and their families. We found out about theater performances and speakers at our local community college, which had a large deaf population. A Deaf Awareness Week scheduled only weeks after we moved, proved to be a wonderful networking opportunity. We felt very supported and welcomed as a family with a cultural need. I lost fifteen pounds!

During the first month of school we invited several families and professionals to our home for a pot luck supper. To our surprise and delight, 45 people showed up! New friends helped us locate our audiologist, a cheap source of batteries, respite care services, telephone relay information, and the free fire detector. We even found someone to help us connect the doorbell to our new kitchen light fixture. Asking questions and tracking down good suggestions was beginning to pay off.

We attended our first staffing the week before school started. It was small, manageable, and friendly. We asked at that meeting what sign system would be used with our child. When told it was the Signing Exact English (SEE II) system, I held up the yellow SEE II dictionary to confirm the response. The speech-language pathologist at the school assured us that she used the same system that the teachers of the deaf and the interpreters used. Our family would need to change the Signed English sign system that we had been using but at least we would be signing the same system at home as would be signed for the next seven years with our daughter at school. Sign consistency -- something we could not obtain in Illinois. We also were told that the previously segregated morning classroom for deaf preschoolers was to be integrated with three hearing children from deaf families. And, Mary Pat would also be programmed for a full day! Kent and I smiled at each other and began to start a new life.

Advocating

In Illinois and Kansas we set goals and expectations for ourselves as family members. We tried to be cooperative, creative, and friendly to the school team but we learned in Illinois that our goals for Mary Pat were not always shared with those who cared for her each day. Other parents assured us that the situation would improve as she got older. I have to agree that it has and it's hard to know how much impact our move to Kansas has had on that fact. Our most important job was to raise Mary Pat and advocate for her within the system. No one else could do it as well as we could while trying to stay well informed and politely assertive. We tried to be watchful that her IEP goals were in fact being carried out. And we communicated frequently with other parents and deaf adults for the support that we continue to need.

Although we were slow to jump into the public school arena to advocate for Mary Pat in Kansas, there were a few issues that we worked on the first year. I was concerned that the fire alarms were not accessible to the deaf and hard-of-hearing staff and children that attended our neighborhood school. We were also amazed that sign classes were not offered to local families. We set to work discussing these issues with the principal, who proved to work slowly but productively until, later that spring, both concerns were resolved. We contemplated forming a parents of deaf children group and decided that because there was one meeting at the school for the deaf and one meeting in the Kansas City area, this was not needed. We decided to encourage other families to drive with us to the monthly meetings, child care provided, that were about a 30 mile drive into a suburb of Kansas City. Only one parent ever accepted, but we enjoyed the chance to chat as we commuted, supporting our families as we brainstormed solutions to problems, and began to make our first real friend.

Basically, as we moved into our new situation in Kansas, we felt like parents of all children feel. We wanted to see our daughter grow into a healthy productive adult with full access to the society around her and able to eventually live on her own, marrying if she desired, and supporting herself in our community. Her special needs had become our own, woven tightly into the fabric of our family. We hoped that Mary Pat would look back as an adult at how we had raised her and educated her and that she would approve. It was with that thought in mind that we moved through the school year.

A Cochlear Implant

The summer that we had moved from Illinois to Kansas I had attended the A. G. Bell conference in Washington D.C. and Mary Pat had gone with me. At one point in the conference, we joined colleagues who were from the Indiana University School of Medicine during a social hour. Mary Pat seemed to captivate the group with her aggressive conversational style, and although she was profoundly deaf, it was clear that she had strong English skills, active parent involvement, and enjoyed wearing her hearing aids. However, her speech was still unintelligible and although she knew that sounds could be loud and soft or long and short, she was not making significant progress in speech and audition.

At four years of age, Mary Pat could not detect her spoken name from across the room, hear the microwave and the vacuum cleaner, or imitate some vowel sounds. We had concerns about her speech development but she had an assertive personality and was as independent as any other preschooler. We had begun to drop some of our signing in familiar routine phrases. For example, we would say things like, (sign and voice) "Do you want..." and then with voice only, "milk or juice." Sometimes we would cover our mouth to see if she could understand a simple sentence that we did not sign. Sometimes she could but if she asked us to sign and not use oral-only communication, we did so immediately. Mary Pat willingly played our speech and audition games...but she just didn't have much hearing. Her speech remained largely unintelligible even to those who were familiar with it.. She had had basically the same speech and audition goals and objectives for two years.

I mentioned to my friends at the conference that it was tiresome sometimes to have to run after Mary Pat to get her attention and that I had always wished that we could try a tactile device. In the past, professionals had advised against it because of her small size and the weight of the equipment, and the fact that she was already wearing personal aids and an FM trainer at school. How much equipment can you put on a petite, preschool child?

In September, 1990, shortly after we had moved and were back from the conference, the telephone rang as we were unpacking boxes. One of the staff at the Indiana University School of Medicine, Amy Robbins, invited us to participate in a research project. Mary Pat, then four years old, would be evaluated by their team in Indianapolis and perhaps was a candidate to wear a seven channel vibral tactile aid for an extended period of time. There were only eight children in the country with this new device. It seemed like a great opportunity to us and we agreed to participate in the evaluation.

In October, Kent, Mary Pattie and I were flown to Indianapolis for three days. We hadn't spent this much time alone with our youngest daughter since we went to meet her for the first time in Texas prior to her adoption two years earlier. We left the other two hearing children with a capable respite care worker and viewed the testing as a holiday away from unpacking and work. Mary Pat was tested by the Indianapolis team on a multitude of speech, English language, and listening tasks while we sought information about research on the new vibral tactile aids. The research team was involved with comparing the communication abilities of children who were using their residual hearing and personal aids, those who had cochlear implants, and those who were using the new seven channel tactile aids. We were told on this visit that Mary Pat was an excellent candidate for a cochlear implant.   However, never having thought much about that option, we discarded it in our enthusiasm for the Tact Aid VII.

Mary Pat was fitted for the tactile aid and we began to watch her closely to see what sounds she felt. The device was worn like a bra across her chest and was connected to a fairly heavy processor that she wore on her waist. We were amazed that the vain little girl was willing to don this equipment. On the way home from dinner on the first night she wore it, she fell asleep with it on. We removed it when we changed her clothes and put her to bed. The next morning, Mary Pat came yelling into our hotel room. She thought someone had taken her new equipment and wanted it back badly. In a flash we realized that there would be no problem with her wearing the Tact Aid!

Mary Pat learned to detect sound with the tactile aid. Three months later, we could call her and she would turn around and attend to us. This might seem like a small feat but anyone who has raised a deaf child can imagine the relief of not having to run after our daughter every single time we wanted to tell her something.   We had become experts at fashioning a comfortable harness for the array of vibrators on her chest so it would fit a little person her size. We relaxed a bit more when she was out in traffic.

In January, she was five years old and we had her speech evaluated at Boy's Town National Research Hospital in Omaha, Nebraska. The clinician, Mary Pat Moeller, was very complimentary of her progress to date and the strategies employed by the speech and language pathologist at her school. But the bottom line was that Mary Pat's speech was largely still unintelligible.

In April, Amy Robbins came from Indianapolis to reevaluate Mary Pat's use of the Tact Aid VII. Kent and I had decided that positive changes with it confirmed by the clinician's objective testing would provide us for a rationale concerning a cochlear implant. We were unprepared to find out that Mary Pat had made no progress at all! She was limited by the capabilities of the tactile aid which only allowed her to detect sound. Her ability to identify and comprehend sound had not changed from what she was capable of doing in October with her two personal aids. After the testing we carefully reviewed Harlan Lane's article about cochlear implants which discussed the National Association of the Deaf position and protest of them, and asked Amy about the data from the Indianapolis research team cited in the Lane article.

Dr. Lane is neither deaf nor a parent of a deaf child and Amy's research-based answers to my questions confirmed that cochlear implant surgery should be seriously considered by us as Mary Pat's parents. I am a researcher myself and had followed the research of Dr. Mary Jo Osberger in Indiana for years. I needed to make a decision based on evidence. I called the institute performing cochlear implants in our community the next day and scheduled an introductory consultation.

For the rest of the spring the implant became a question largely influenced by insurance and consideration of Mary Pat's esteem as a deaf citizen. Meanwhile I had heard of a deaf woman at Gallaudet that had been implanted. She didn't wear the equipment to work because she was surrounded there by those who signed. Yet, when she was off campus in the hearing world, she found the device useful. "Oh," I thought, impressed by that story, "the best of both worlds." I had attended a deaf culture conference in Texas in March and talked to several deaf adults about cochlear implants. They told me that in their opinion I was not accepting my daughter's deafness and they asked me why I was trying to "fix her." It was challenging to listen to them. Yet, I did not feel that my perception of Mary Pat had changed as I considered the implant. Mary Pat was, is and always will be a deaf person--but not all deaf people are profoundly deaf as was Mary Pat. One of the women voicing her opinion had excellent speech; better speech than we ever dreamed Mary Pat would have. Kent and I wanted to raise a bilingual/bicultural daughter. She already could sign in both English and ASL. How would the implant change that?

A week later I sat crying silently through a Quaker Meeting for worship. I was tormented by the decision. It had gone on too long. I knew almost too much about deafness! After meeting a doctor, our friend Lydia Moore, made an analogy that was helpful to me. She explained that some people have artificial hip implants. Several people, she said, are implanted with an artificial hip, have therapy, exercise and do very well. Others ignored the artificial hip and make no visible change in their behavior. The analogy to me meant that even if we implanted Mary Pat and she hated what we had done when she matured, she could just take the equipment off and not use it. Without the external microphone and processor no one would know she had had cochlear implant surgery.

We decided to interview deaf adults who had had cochlear implants as we made our decision. I got the names of both pleased and dissatisfied users from two different clinics and wrote a basic letter to each person. I asked about the most positive the most negative aspect about the operation. I asked if they would have it done again to themselves and I asked that if they were to become a parent of deaf children, would they elect to have the surgery for their child. I received about two dozen replies, all very positive. All would do it again; all would have done it for their son or daughter.

Later that month, Kent, Mary Pat, and I visited the home of a local deaf teacher, a man raised orally who had been implanted for about two years. It was an insightful evening.

He invited us to ask him any question. We asked about the pain of the surgery, what he could initially hear, what he heard now. He let us see his scar and Mary Pat felt it. She asked questions of her own. Recalling his stories brings tears to my eyes again. He told about hearing his daughter's voice for the first time and how birds sounded to him now. He explained that after two years there were still subtle sounds that he was learning to identify.

About a week later, we invited a young deaf woman and her two hearing children to dinner with us. Her name had been given me by a strong ASL advocate at the residential school. Despite his personal philosophy, he wanted to help us. The woman had had the single channel implant surgery when she was about 18 years old and had just recently had it replaced with the 22 channel device. She was interesting to talk to indeed! She could tell us the difference between the two types of devices. Where once she had been able to hear her children talking, now she could tell the difference in their young voices. Where once she knew that the radio was on, now she could tell the type of music that was playing. She could use the device to tell her that conversation was starting and stopping during meetings so that she could gain the floor and make comments without interrupting. She was very positive about the device and her equipment which was much smaller than the vibral tactile equipment that Mary Pat was now wearing. Most importantly, this woman explained, similar to the story I had heard about the Gallaudet woman, that when she was around deaf people she took the device off. For some reason this option made the surgery palatable to me.

Work obligations and a rigid schedule prevented Kent from being able to visit the institute with me for our first consultation about the implant surgery. I felt as if the weight of the world was on my shoulders as I sat in the meeting and wished Kent had had enough sick or personal days left to join me. I felt disappointed that the staff would not schedule the appointment for later in the day so that we both could have attended as parents. Once again, we were asking for a family perspective.

The decision was difficult to make. The video tapes and information I was shown were all too unscientific. Everyone, they seemed to claim, would benefit. I knew from my own investigation that this was not true. I called back to our friends in Indianapolis soon after and reviewed Mary Pat's situation with them. Because of their frank, empirical information and their knowledge of our specific child, we decided to schedule the surgery.

Two days before Mary Pat was admitted for surgery, a deaf adult, highly respected in our community, expressed his disappointment about our decision. Was she a guinea pig, he wanted to know? I sent Kent alone to sign the release forms and hear about all that could go wrong with the surgery the day before it occurred. I was shaken, tired, and exhausted.

I was scared about Mary Pat's forthcoming surgery. None of my children had ever had major surgery, but Amy Robbins had told me that many parents of, for example, meningitic children have been through such invasive medical procedures that the implant seems like simple surgery to them. Yet, this was elective surgery. It was but three days prior to the operation that the insurance company put in writing that they would cover it: all expenses after we paid our maximum copayment of $500. We felt like we had just saved thousands of dollars, having expected to have to pay 20% of the $30,000 bill up until that day.

Due to the pressure of work, I worked the morning of Mary Pat's surgery and met her and Kent at the hospital in the late morning. She was loving all the attention. We had told her all that we could about what was to happen. We videotaped some segments of her explaining her understanding of the surgery to us. She had a very good friend Michael who had been implanted so she had seen his equipment and his scar often, and she trusted us on her behalf. Next I videotaped her in the hospital room with her surgical cap on talking to the anesthesiologist and as she was rolled out to surgery.

As we waited, we talked with another couple whose son Eddie was there for surgery as well. Once an assistant came up to inform us that things were going well. The time went quickly but painfully. I wondered several times if I could stop them, tell them I had changed my mind---but then she was done and we were called. Kent carried her to her room in his big arms, her head wrapped in a turban of bandages.

When we got to Mary Pat's room, we were pleased to discover that Eddie was right next door. We visited and checked on each other's children throughout the afternoon. Mary Pat was in mild discomfort for about three hours, sitting up, whining, sliding back down, asking for ice, not wanting it. I began to tell her long stories of the Three Little Pigs, Goldilocks and the Three Bears and such until she finally fell asleep. The anesthesiologist came by to tell us how well both children did. It was a relief to talk to him. I left to go home to Breeze and Hannah for dinner. We were supposed to go to a movie as a special treat that night but we decided to visit Mary Pat instead.

What a great decision. We were greeted at the hospital by Eddie, age three, in a wheelchair zooming up and down the halls looking happy and alert. Upstairs we found Mary Pat still asleep but when we awoke her to tell her about Eddie, she too wanted a wheelchair ride. She was her old self again just eight hours after surgery! The girls and I stayed for about an hour. There were flowers from friends at the Kansas School for the Deaf and from Michael. A family friend called. We left Kent and Mary Pat for the one night that she was required to stay in the hospital. Everyone slept well.

The next morning I passed her doctor in the hall as I walked off the elevator. He was pleased with her recovery and said she could go home as soon as she was ready. As I entered the room she and Kent were packing her things. She hadn't eaten for 36 hours and was starved. So we waited for breakfast and then walked out together. I returned to work until noon and then called to see how they were doing. Oh, she was fine; in fact, she was bored. To give Kent a chance for a nap, I drove home to take her for a visit at school. Everyone was thrilled to see her--especially Michael. He signed and signed about the similarities of her shaven patch of hair and his memory of his surgery. What was to be a short visit continued a couple of hours until school was dismissed. The staff at school were some of the only friends we had, and it was a fine feeling to have their support as we interrupted the academic day. We were all so relieved that the surgery was over, we just had to share it with someone! Because it was the Memorial Day weekend, it was three days before Mary Pat returned to school. We had to wait a month for the hookup.

Mary Pat was hooked up in June, 1991. They programmed all 22 channels. I thought I wouldn't cry when she first heard sound because I had seen it on videotapes of other children. But I did. Mary Pat was so excited and cooperative. Yes, yes, she could definitely hear those sounds! At home she was the Helen Keller of the cochlear implant. She went from water faucet to toilet, making noises and laughing. Within days she could hear the telephone, the doorbell, and her name called from all over the house.

Kent and the other girls took her to Indianapolis in June for testing. She responded well to the evaluation, improving on her speech and audition scores dramatically compared to her previous two sets of data. Kent learned a lot of new information about auditory training and bought her some new toys that made sound. He was empowered by the team who provided him with many helpful hints about how to use the new implant. A week later, I joined my family at Quaker camp in the mountains of North Carolina for vacation. During those weeks we played Go Fish and had some short conversational exchanges without sign. By the time we met up with Grandma Bette in Florida, two weeks later, Mary Pat was able to make several conversational exchanges about a familiar topic without sign. This was her first real conversation with her grandma and it was a Kodak moment! Mary Pat listened for new sounds and delighted in naming the ones she had learned to recognize. She could say Hannah and Breeze with much more clarity; Mama was perfect.

We were anxious for school to start that fall and for professionals who knew her to have the opportunity to see the changes in her speech and hearing. In preparation for the start of school, I took her to her first audiological appointment since the surgery. Having sat in countless booths with my daughter over the past three years, I was shocked when she was able to detect speech at 10 decibels. She appeared to have an almost flat 45 decibel loss out to 8,000 Hz. Even though I knew this only meant she could detect sound (not comprehend speech) at these levels, I asked the audiologist to please call the institute and check if this was even possible. Yes, it was confirmed. As I sat and listened to the professionals talk over the phone and tried to digest the information, I took a whole new completely positive attitude about the implant.

English Language Intervention

Mary Pat had no comprehensible language available to her until she was two and a half years old. To make up for lost time, we immersed her in signing at home and school. But in addition, I began to read the literature on research-based language intervention strategies. Few of these strategies had been empirically studied with deaf children, so I combined them with intuition and family needs, and set out to see what was workable. Through the first three years of the time that we had Mary Pat, we relied heavily on an assessment notebook, the <u>Developmental Language Curriculum; A Comprehensive Guide and Record-Keeping System for Hearing-Impaired Students, Infant Through Twelve Years</u> (Cheney, Compton, and Harder, 1988). Broken down by six month intervals, literally hundreds of English language skills are listed, and appendices of adjectives, double verbs, idiomatic expressions, and so forth, can be referenced in the back. We would choose several appropriate language targets from this book, incorporate them into our lives, take great pride when the girls demonstrate their understanding or use of them, and would set new goals. In this manner, our language environment was always slightly more advanced than Mary Pat's. Once we moved to Kansas, the preschool teacher worked closely with me in this process, such that many of the goals became IEP goals as well.

We never drilled Mary Pat on language patterns. Instead, we would choose language goals, say for example, use of the connective "and", and we would use it as much as possible in our activities. In the morning, when Mary Pat was dressing, I might sign, "Get your shoes AND socks" or while packing her lunch, "Do you want peanut butter AND jelly--or just peanut butter?"

From the start, we expected Mary Pat to be a communicator. If we ask a question, we would expect an answer. If we didn't get an answer, we would prompt "yes or no?" When Mary Pat first came to live with us, we would match her non-linguistic communication with signs and pretend we could not understand until she used language to communicate with us. For at least a year, I would supervise the other family members, taking pains to see that Mary Pat was expected to sign in addition to her mime, cow eye stares, and theatrical antics. By the end of her first year, she could hold her own in a conversation about a topic and make several turns in conversation. Her dialogues included long strings of gestures mixed with signs and the facial expressions that might someday win her a role with the National Theater of the Deaf and almost always made us giggle. But we believed in her ability to communicate, and she came to see the joy and power that shared language can afford.

We would never solve a problem too fast, obtain a desired object too quickly, or respond too agreeably to a request around the house. Sometimes, we would purposely skip Mary Pat's turn in an activity or serving of food, "forget" the rules to a game, or pretend to use a utensil or tool inappropriately. These occasions gave her opportunities to use the language that she had acquired, feel control and pride in our home, and expand her conversational skills. Sometimes you could almost see her thinking of how to put her signs or her speech and signs together. Later, we observed the same need for time when Mary Pat would try to articulate carefully. Often we would have to remind each other, "wait, wait--let her try; give her a chance." In our busy lives, it was a conscious decision to make language learning a priority. And it was! For me, building an age-appropriate first language base was the number one priority that I held for Mary Pat.

I had read that if we as adult language users would utilize specific language strategies we might actually be able to accelerate the English language acquisition of our deaf daughter. One strategy was to incorporate partial repetitions of my own preceding utterance. I might say something like, "Put it here, Mary Pat -- beside the other one." Then, if I thought she didn't understand the word "beside", use partial repetitions: "Put it here, <u>next to</u> the orange one. That's right, right here, <u>beside</u> this one. Yes, you got it, <u>beside it</u>." We would also encourage Mary Pat to imitate our comments. This was not supported by what I read, but it gave me satisfaction to see that she retained a target phrase long enough to repeat it back. The imitation component eventually integrated into the conversation so that it never seemed contrived.

Breeze, Kent, and I all became masterful "expanders" of what Mary Pat said and signed. If she asked for "milk," we might clarify, "Oh, you want milk?" If Mary Pat said, "I want a banana" as I was packing her lunch, I might expand it to "Oh, you want the last banana for lunch?" Because we reviewed the <u>Developmental Language Curriculum</u> frequently, I was often able to include a target that I knew was emerging in her language.

From the beginning, we built on simple home routines. First we would label the nouns of everything. When Mary Pat could do that, we would expect some simple carrier phrases to be used. "I want cereal." "I need milk" are early examples. We would model them or incorporate them into our half of the dialogue until Mary Pat used them appropriately. After that, we'd ask for the kind of cereal and buy chocolate milk so there was a choice. When it was time for color words, I made sure we had several attractive cups of different colors. Later, I asked if she wanted a plastic or metal spoon or a paper or aluminum cup. And on and on, until Mary Pat saw the control she could achieve with language. We built on teethbrushing, packing lunches, changing clothes, using the bathroom, doing errands in the same manner.

By the time Mary Pat entered first grade, I was very conscientiously NOT changing my thoughts as I communicated with her. That is, I purposely used figurative expressions and hard vocabulary. We began to fingerspell lots of words and always turn on the decoder on the television set.

Changes With the Implant

Mary Pat's understanding of the sounds she was hearing continued to improve. She could hear her sisters whispering, the microwave bell, the hum of the refrigerator. One day in October, Hannah and I were singing simple songs in the front of the car and Mary Pat identified one from the back seat. This totally shocked me and for the next week or so it became our routine to sing on the way to school. The first time we did this, Mary Pat got one of three songs identified correctly. On the second day, it was four; five on the third day! We started to teach her a variety of children's songs, new nursery rhymes, and words for which there were no signs. We expanded her realm of child culture. Soon she was reading, sounding out words, and using a phonics approach. This was important for the then kindergartener. I could simply read stories to her without signs, sitting beside her on the couch. I could understand almost everything she said to me if I knew the topic. A whole other kind of world was opening up to her. One day, out of the blue, she said to me, "I love that I am deaf, I love my cochlear implant." Months ago, I would have found these two statements contradictory, but now I saw clearly that my daughter was learning both English and American Sign Language and had both deaf and hearing friends. She could be both a deaf person and make good use of her hearing and speech abilities.

In December, we traveled to Omaha for a re-evaluation of Mary Pat's speech skills. It had been six months since she had been hooked up but we felt we were too subjective about the changes in her speech. We thought it was improving but we wanted objective testing to confirm this as well as to

identify priorities for speech production training. Some of the results of testing that day were that
-- Mary Pat had previously deleted final consonants, she now rarely did so when speaking single words;
-- syllable reduction observed in January was now only rarely observed;
-- single word production had increased markedly in its intelligibility;
-- conversational speech was still difficult to understand for the unfamiliar listener;
-- it was encouraging to see Mary Pat's progress with her cochlear implant and to know how she corrected herself when provided a spoken model.

Kindergarten for Mary Pat

Mary Pat was the only deaf child integrated into a room of about 20 hearing kindergartners. She had a flexible, assertive, creative general education kindergarten teacher, Mrs. Ross, who had previous experience with deaf children in her room and had worked with an interpreter. Both Kent and I observed the situation initially in the fall, not to visit again until spring.

Our principal had told interpreters the previous spring that if they were not willing to sign in English he was not interested in employing them the following fall. For that reason, the school started to fall short several interpreters. As parents we were appreciative of the school's effort to sign consistently among staff but we were also concerned that Mary Pat was not given access to all the conversation and teacher language about her. It was a trade off. We needed to be patient. Mary Pat's interpreter had been a paraprofessional in her preschool classroom in the years before. That summer she had attended a two-week intensive sign workshop and although her sign skills were not expert or polished she was willing to sign in English, looked up signs constantly and could not have been more well-intended or motivated. Also in that year, the administration supported the evaluation of interpreter sign skills. All the interpreters participated. This was a positive step, and one few schools have taken to date.

An advisory committee was also set up the year Mary Pat was in kindergarten. It included members of the deaf community, parents from other programs, and parents, teachers and interpreters from our program. There were strengths and needs reflected in the program for deaf or hard of hearing children in our school. We still were nervous about observing there but we began to realize that our worries were unnecessary. The members of our team were honest about their knowledge of a topic, eager to try new ideas and materials, usually willing to attend conferences to gain new insights, and so forth. Our staffings no longer kept us up at night and we didn't wait until our annual meeting if we wanted to discuss a need with our team. Often, Kent and I would alternate our attendance at meetings, a symbol that we trusted those with whom Mary Pat spent seven hours of their day. Mary Pat's needs became intertwined with Hannah's needs for extra hugs and assurance, Breeze's needs for special privileges, my need for quiet time, and so forth. The special needs of all our children became our own, woven tightly into the fabric of our family.

Signing to a Six Year Old

A definite challenge for us as parents was to continually introduce new words and expressions using authentic English to Mary Pat and not limiting ourselves to only those phrases for which we knew the signs. We began to invent and record signs in a computer data base for common foods like "Wheat

Chex" and "chicken nuggets", places in the community, household items like "grater" and "detergent", clothing like "tuck" and "cuff", etc., and show and tell topics like, "Teenage Mutant Ninja Turtles." Mary Pat's sisters took the responsibility of teaching their sister "children culture words and expressions," such as "nerd" and "dork," and names of TV shows and characters. Staff at her school did likewise with basal reader and unit words. We shared our words and recorded them as a team. We kept our list in our SEE II dictionary.

We also asked Mary Pat to teach us the signs that she was using at school. When discussing hot lunch, I would ask her questions such as, "Now, how do you sign hamburger <u>bun</u> at school?" This is a strange situation for parents of deaf kids: asking them for information, giving them responsibilities atypical of those given to other young children. I felt equally uneasy when we'd occasionally check with Mary Pat if she wanted to attend residential school or wear an FM unit. Did other six year olds make such decisions? How much stock should we put in her replies? Hmmm....

Beginning Literacy

About this same time we set up a VCR in Mary Pat's room and allowed her to watch videotaped stories before she went to sleep. For years we had allowed our older daughters to listen to audio tapes at bedtime, so we thought that this similar activity was appropriate for Mary Pat. Finding few videotapes available in Signed English and none available in Exact English, we made some ourselves and purchased others.

Because of some research I had been doing with colleagues at Gallaudet University, I was aware of the importance of environment print for decoding reading materials. We would call Mary Pat's attention to letters and numbers that appeared on t-shirts, food packaging, and sign boards. In Illinois, a local restaurant owner, Louie, let us create a new version of his children's menu adding signs for all the foods to the printed words. Then, as young customers, both hearing and deaf waited for their orders, they could learn to sign hamburger and french fry at the Kings Way Restaurant. Five years later the menu is still in use.

The rewards for all this reading, signing, and conversation, became apparent. Mary Pattie used long, complicated sentences, speaking and signing in figurative English: "My nose is runny," "I stepped on a step," "I dropped my lemon drop." At four years of age, she was saying things like, "I want to ask my teacher if I can be a ballerina in my class". It was somewhat disheartening that some professionals would attribute her language to intelligence, early identification (2-1/2 years old?), and residual hearing (profound deafness until age 5?) instead of collected group effort. We believe that Mary Pat was making the literacy progress she was because we signed to her just as hearing parents would speak to children; the grammar and syntax of English were accessible. And because our home was filled with books, computers, and notes written in haste about groceries and schedules. Signing in English, she used the sign markers for plural and possessive -S, -Y, past tense, -IST (dentist) and -ISH (redish) quite consistently. Markers such as these were listed among her IEP objectives and the adults in her environment tried to model them consistently.

Mary Pat worked on the computer almost daily as did everyone else in the family at that time. She enjoyed using software called Muppetville (which we signed as M forming town) and on her own she selected and operated several programs from the menu. She also liked an Apple program called Mousepaint that let her use a mouse to draw and erase. She would spend 15 to 30 minutes a day working

48

independently on the computer. One day, as a neighbor friend, Alan, was working with her on the computer, he learned his first signed phrases, "move over, my turn, stop." Breeze evaluated Mary Pat on a number of computer software programs and eventually wrote an article that she co-authored about her work. It was published in 1992, in the Perspectives magazine and provided the strengths and weaknesses of about a dozen software programs.

Deaf Culture

When Mary Pat first started school in Olathe, we did not take immediate advantage of the residential school that was in our community. I had taken Mary Pat to visit there twice, once to eat dinner and once to socialize after school when we first moved. But when we were more settled, we asked that she attend two afternoons a week and stay after school and for dinner. We valued her contact with other deaf children and deaf adults at the school, and we felt that she was ready to learn conceptual sign.

That first year was a rough one in terms of convincing her that KSD was a good place to spend some time. In the years that followed, she seemed to feel more comfortable there and began make friends. It became more comfortable for us also to walk through the dorm halls, chat with the staff, talk about our children and the other children at the school, and feel that this resource was a valuable part of our community. Occasional parent meetings, an annual weekend conference for families, the Winter Holiday program, and similar activities became regular events for our family. "Oh," Hannah proclaimed as a third grader on one such visit, "I wish I were deaf!"

It hasn't been as easy as one might think to establish strong relationships with deaf adults in Kansas. Back in

Illinois, in a small town with few residents who were deaf, we had arranged monthly social meetings with the few deaf adults and children that we found in our rural community, dining out together, going bowling and arranging picnics and birthday parties. Two of these couples were considerably older; we began to think of them as Mary Pat's adopted grandparents. One couple, the Troegers, came with us as family on the day we officially adopted Mary Pat. Along with our shared activities, they also took her along to deaf social events in neighboring towns. The time commitment that this involved for our family was amply repaid by the warmth and respect that we found at these social gatherings.

In Kansas, when Mary Pat began to attend school with hearing children of deaf families reverse mainstreamed into her class, we were provided with families to socialize with on the weekends. We had something in common: our children and we would often chat as we dropped them off to play or when we came to pick them up. Occasionally we would have deaf adults over for dinner. Usually these were young college students or deaf people who had recently graduated from college. Everyone seemed to enjoy socializing around dinner, chatting with the children, talking about the adoption of deaf children, helping us figure out better ways to use our assistive listening devices, and so on. Although we found these events somewhat awkward to plan, we honestly told deaf adults that our objective was for our children to socialize with them. This straightforward attitude seemed to pay off well because the deaf adults that we invited to our home would spend quality time with our children before dinner. Finding opportunities to genuinely socialize with deaf adults still challenges our family. We have suggested Saturday morning storytelling at the residential school for both hearing families and deaf families, family nights at the Deaf Club, and the idea of deaf families adopting hearing families in our community to share time together. None of these particular ideas have become materialized.

The Arts

Once settled in Kansas our older girls found Suzuki violin teachers. This had been a regular routine in our home back in Illinois and although it took us a while to get started in Kansas, we welcomed the consistency that this activity brought to our lives. Suzuki violin involves private lessons, group performances and individual time with parents at home. The method afforded Kent and me special time with each of our hearing children, although Breeze, by now a member of the Kansas City Youth Symphony, had progressed past needing us much.

Although we felt that this was an important activity in which we engaged each day, we realized as Mary Pat got older she too needed some creative artistic outlet. She had wanted to purchase a plastic violin. She was communicating her need to also have some special activity of her own. We looked at ballet classes, karate classes, art classes, before settling on gymnastics. Even though she was younger than our hearing children when they started after school activities, we felt that it was important for her to have some outside activity in which she could physically excel in an artistic manner. In fourth grade we added jazz.

Interpreting

We had no complaints in our family when we expected everyone to sign everything they said to Mary Pat. If the older girls were tired or not feeling well, we would interpret for them--not in an overt way, but by simply beginning to sign as they talked to us. Almost immediately on such occasions, if we began interpreting, they would raise their hands and continue to sign for themselves, rather than wait for interpretation. By the time Breeze was 12 years old, other parents of deaf children were hiring her to sign for sports events. It sure beat being paid a menial wage to babysit! At school, Breeze interpreted the announcements, lunch conversations, and songs to friends who attended the Junior High from KSD. That same year, Breeze interpreted for Mary Pat for an entire weekend at a national women's music festival. She felt humbled as she learned the ropes of a full day interpreting job and yet took pride in the information that Mary Pat retained from the weekend.

Even though everyone in our family could sign most anything they wanted to say, it is obvious to them when Kent or I cannot interpret. Maybe we'd be making cookies and my hands were busy or I would be loading the dishwasher or packing lunches as we got ready for school. I'd call to Hannah to translate, and she did so easily, probably because she realized that I sincerely needed her help. We might have been carrying groceries to the car and I yelled to Breeze to tell Mary Pat to stay close as we walked through the parking lot. Or we would be walking down the aisles of a clothing store, the children ahead or behind me, unable to see my signing hands or hear my voice. I might have been upstairs and the three girls downstairs. My hands might have been busy with my briefcase and books while theirs were free to sign. We thought it was logical that the girls would be willing to interpret in these family situations and we expected and rewarded them verbally for doing so. Whatever the situation, the older girls have always accepted their participation in our family as potential signers when needed.

After returning from Deaf Way at Gallaudet University in 1989, we all agreed to sign everything we said no matter to whom, in the kitchen--the hot spot of our home. We planned to add an additional room to this rule each year until we covered the whole house but that plan was never actualized. Originally, the idea of signing only in the kitchen gave our hearing girls some flexibility and an occasional needed break from concentrating on signing. Hannah especially would actually step out of the kitchen at unannounced times during conversations when she was between five and ten years of age. We felt that this option was important for our young family members. As a group, we hearing family members are still not very good at signing when we are busy, tired, or angry about something, but we tried to model these moods as much as is humanly possible so that there is access to a variety of emotions.

Complete English Signing

As a parent and educator, I was grateful to the Olathe administration that they had financed an occasional series of evening sign classes for community members, and interested shop keepers attended these classes. In the fall of 1992, sign classes were taught as a regular part of the school day to all the classes at the elementary school where Mary Pat and about a dozen other children who were deaf or hard of hearing attended school. This meant that the children could socialize more easily and had communicative access. Unlike the generation that preceded them, these students were are growing up in a new age--one in which events were interpreted, television was captioned, and family and friends saw nothing wrong with signing.

I was also pleased the Olathe public school had a policy as to sign system use in the deaf education program. It had been in place for at least three years before we moved to Olathe, and had been the reason we had chosen to move into this school district. Administrators had chosen SEE II prior to our coming to the Olathe area because of their belief that it would more clearly teach young people how to read, speak and write. The administrators believed that SEE II gave deaf students a basic foundation of English and that ASL was available at the Kansas School for the Deaf.

We were not competent SEE II signers and still are not to this day, but my research had demonstrated that when groups of deaf children were exposed to models of English signed by teachers in a complete and consistent manner, they scored significantly higher on tests of reading and English skills than those whose teachers signed conceptually. This research, repeated several times with slight changes in methodology over a period of four years, showed that SEE systems, Cued Speech, and Oral English--when understood by children--were all equally successful. There was no research to support the notion that deaf children needed to learn "concepts first." They were just as smart as hearing people and they were perfectly capable of learning literal English if that is what they had seen and were exposed to as their language developed.

However, deaf children could learn neither ASL nor English unless they had an opportunity to see it used completely, comprehensibly, and consistently. The use of Signed English or Pidgin Sign English (contact signing) might have legitimate purposes outside the classroom, but there was no empirical evidence at all to show that deaf children could acquire mature forms of ASL or English when exposed to these models that did not represent the grammer of either language.

In the spring there had been confrontation in our community about the use of SEE II in the public school. Several professionals from the Kansas School for the Deaf unhappy about the sign choice had met with administrators of the public school system. To the deaf adults, the use of SEE II totally rejected their culture. Meetings were held throughout the spring with different people voicing different opinions on the issue. Eventually, an advisory committee was formed so that the discussions could continue. New signs needing to be invented could be discussed with deaf adults and signs that the deaf community found offensive could be altered.

It was hard for me to be a parent in Olathe during this discussion because I was a professional in Kansas City. I attended most of the meetings that involved the sign system issue until summer came along and my time was required elsewhere. I did write what I considered one compelling letter to the editor of our Olathe newspaper during this time. I stated in that letter, that most importantly American Sign Language was a comprehensible, complete, consistent language. It had all the prestige that English had. I thought that deaf adults and hearing children of deaf adults working in schools who were proficient at ASL should be allowed to use it with deaf children. They had been oppressed for far too long and it was their right to use their language at school and to have it used in interpreting situations in the community. I stated that I believed that ASL would never die as some deaf adults feared. It had been around since the first deaf people living in America and remained through years of oral suppression and I believed it would last forever. But I also stated that there was no reason why deaf children could not learn both ASL and English. In fact, many deaf citizens in that community were bilingual, signing both ASL and English. But most deaf children, I knew from my work, knew neither language well and, therefore, didn't read well either. They were the children continually instructed in sign systems that were neither pure ASL nor complete English. I said in my letter that there were three ways to learn two languages: 1) Learn both at the same time from adults, some of who were using one complete form of one language and some of whom were using one complete form of another language; 2) learn ASL and then English, and 3) learn English and then ASL. The deaf children at our school were learning English from their teachers and parents. This was reasonable given that they were from hearing families and their parents and siblings signed English at home and that their teachers and educational interpreters didn't know ASL. They could learn American Sign Language at KSD after school or later in their lives.

Many positive things came out of the discussions about signing that spring in Kansas. A year after the advisory board was in place, the issue had calmed down considerably. Signing in Exact English was respected in the public school program and the Kansas School for the Deaf was busy trying to increase their use of ASL. Children were being educated in both schools, and, in some cases, children spent a half day in one program and a half day in the other. This residential school was considered a rich resource in our community that exposed deaf children of hearing families to opportunities that they would not have had had the residential school and the deaf adults who lived in our community not been such a viable force.

Respite Care

Our family had long been users of respite care. Although we were middle class people, we found it difficult to afford babysitters who could interpret well for Mary Pat. In daycare situations, we thought it unfortunate that we were expected to pay for both childcare and interpreting. In Illinois we had been privy to a wonderful respite care system affording us many hours each month in which we could hire signing college students to babysit our children. There was a similar program in Kansas that benefited our family. When we needed a weekend off once or twice a year, or vacation time alone, we relied on college students with appropriate healthcare skills and basic interpreting knowledge to care for our children. Later, when we investigated the adoption of other deaf children and needed to be away from home on weekends to visit them, we were appreciative of the respite care services that were available to us.

Another post adoption service that was helpful when it could be utilized, was Mary Pat's Medicaid card. It paid for glasses, earmolds, aids, and batteries. We used it at a time when Mary Pat needed a new size of glasses annually and new ear molds every six months. We encouraged families to investigate these supports that might be available to them. Any money saved by use of the card will undoubtedly be needed to pay for interpreters!

Making Friends

By spring of Mary Pat's kindergarten year, it very much concerned Kent and me that she seemed to have no real hearing friends. She spent hours each weekend with her deaf friend Michael, a second grader. Yet, no hearing children invited her to play.

We had experienced several ways in Illinois that friends had tried to learn to sign with our new deaf daughter. Some took sign classes offered for adults and students in the community. For others, we planned a home video tape of survival phrases that circulated throughout our neighborhood. We made a point of donating books and tapes about deafness and communication to our local libraries in both Illinois and Kansas, thanked people for every attempt to learn to sign and continually sought ways to make signing a part of our community. In Kansas, the newness of having adopted Mary Pat long since worn off, we found ourselves less interested in teaching sign classes and it really wasn't necessary since many were offered in the community.

We found that the children who signed to Mary Pat were the children who attended public schools with deaf children. These children naturally had learned to sign, self-selected out of larger classes of hearing children to be those who were particularly interested in communicating with deaf children. Some of the children in Mary Pat's preschool and kindergarten classes would come up and wave their hands at our daughter. We considered it a precursor characteristic of children who would soon learn to sign. Other children were not interested; no matter how much they were exposed to signing, it simply wasn't something they felt comfortable doing. In every class in which deaf children were integrated in our home school, we noticed that there were specific children interested in signing who paid special attention to the interpreters, and sincerely enjoyed friendships with their deaf peers.

Yet, in Mary Pat's kindergarten year we became concerned that Mary Pat was never invited to the homes of any of her hearing friends. When we would invite these friends over, they would play nicely with our daughter (and we marveled at how they could communicate) but they never returned the favor and invited Mary Pat to their home. We observed again at school and then met with the staff that worked with our daughter. We openly expressed our desperation and concern that our daughter seemed to have no real hearing friends at school. We were relieved that the team did not ignore our sincere concerns but took them very seriously. The kindergarten teacher, Ms. Ross, impressed me a great deal with a note she wrote me a few days later expressing her desire, too, that Mary Pat develop real friendships. The team worked together to change the way the interpreter was used during some of the social times at school.

Experimentation continued throughout the rest of the school year.

In our spring staffing, we asked the principal to consider placing various children who had expressed an interest in friendship with Mary Pat in her classroom the following year. Since there might be two or three first grade classrooms, we felt that calling these particular children to his attention could be advantageous to Mary Pat as she progressed through school. We also knew that Hannah, our soon to be fourth grader, was also not utilized as the resource she might have been because of her ability to sign. The three deaf children that were in her grade level were in a different class. We asked that she be educated with them the following year.

We also bought about a dozen books from the Gallaudet University Press that would appeal to young children of Mary Pat's age. They were books about signing, about hearing dogs, about having deaf parents, about how hearing aids worked and about how it felt to be a young deaf person in a public school setting. It was our intention that these books be read to the children and left available for them read on their own. The kindergarten teacher was very accommodating in this regard and sent all the books home when they had been used so that we could recycle them the following year.

When Mary Pat started first grade in the fall, her classroom teacher invited us to speak briefly about her social needs to the parents of the other children in her class of twelve. We did. We invited hearing kids to play on weekends. Everyone at the birthday party that year was hearing. Yet, school staff continued to work with our concern. The speech pathologist suggested that Mary Pat invite a friend to speech sessions on a weekly basis. The kids loved this idea. The teacher of the deaf, who saw Mary Pat and a small group of her hearing classmates, for "small group time," changed her activities so that the hearing children signed more to Mary

Pat. We discussed strategies for making and keeping friendships with Mary Pat at home. By the time she entered fourth grade, friendships were no longer a concern

Marcy

As things started to settle in our lives, we regained our enthusiasm for the adoption of a second deaf child. We realized early on after the adoption of Mary Pat that no matter how skillful we became as signers, we were still a houseful of hearing people with hearing attitudes and beliefs. And we hadn't been adopted either. We needed to balance our family to some degree. We had been looking on and off for approximately four years for a second deaf child. It wasn't any easier the second time around. Sometimes I would contact professional magazines with short letters of appeal. Sometimes I would tackle the social service agencies. It would go in spurts.

By fall, 1991, we had looked seriously at four deaf children. First, an infant deaf child, promised to us from Florida. However, when I went to make the initial first visit, the social agency informed us that the foster family had decided to keep the child. They returned our check with a letter in the mail and without a phone call or any personal explanation. I opened the letter, the check fell out, and I sat and cried. Later on the phone, talking to my mother, she expressed my feelings precisely. "It's as if you had a miscarriage," she said. I waited for Kent and the girls to come home from school. Everyone cried and for days we talked about the little brother we had lost.

Next was a set of twins from Pennsylvania, three years old, deaf, and with heart problems. We changed vacation plans during the summer, spent $1200 in airplane tickets, hotel, and rent-a-cars to visit these children, only to find out in our initial visit with them that they had multiple additional problems. The young social worker who had handled our case had clearly misrepresented these children to us. We left Pennsylvania in total despair, having spent money, time, and effort that was sorely needed elsewhere in our family budget. Finally, we looked at a deaf-blind boy from Korea. The agency wanted a large sum of money for this child despite the fact that he would need at least one eye operation once in our care. We considered his case carefully and talked to a dear friend who is an ophthalmologist and lives near us. We finally decided that with our busy lives and hectic schedules, having a visually-impaired as well as deaf child would not be an appropriate fit. When we found that another family was interested in the little boy, we relinquished our interest in him.

All the children in whom we had expressed an interest were eventually adopted by others. We had just settled back to focus on other aspects of our lives when I got an unexpected call in December, 1991, from an agency in Seattle. They had been placing children from Bulgaria. An adoption had fallen through and they had gotten our name from one of the organizations that I had contacted just several months prior. They had a four year old, deaf girl with severe behavioral problems and who was not adjusting well to her new home in Michigan. They needed an immediate placement. I told them I would call them back.

I got hold of Kent who miraculously was at his desk at school. "Yeah, sure, I feel pregnant," he said after I provided the scant information relayed to me from the agency personnel. I called back and accepted the child. It just felt right.

Kent and I had planned a holiday vacation with our friends, John Luckner and Sue Rudolph. We didn't feel that we should give up this vacation or that we should bring our new daughter back only to put her in respite care. So, we delayed our meeting with her for several weeks. On January 2, 1992, the day after I returned from vacation, I flew to Michigan to meet our fourth daughter. Marcy, as she came to be called by our family, was a healthy four year old profoundly deaf child. She had been raised in an orphanage in Bulgaria and, from information we had received, had never cut, never colored, and had been denied many opportunities that typical four year olds in America enjoy.

Marcy's unacceptable behaviors had already begun to decrease in foster care. However, she still was not sleeping well at night, sucked her thumb continually, often had tantrums, and was uncooperative when she was not in control of situations. She neither kissed nor hugged nor was receptive of kisses or hugs. Marcy continually tested.

I stayed with Marcy for four days in Michigan, snuggling, signing to her and taking her to the mall. We flew home and Kent and the girls met us at the airport. Driving back to Olathe, we decided to stop at the Quaker meeting house to introduce our Meeting to our new daughter. Smiles and hugs all around. Unknown to us, we were going to need the strength of these friendships in the months ahead.

Receiving little administrative support at work for maternity leave, Kent and I were forced to switch off and on days at home for the next several weeks as Marcy adjusted to our home. She started school the day after her arrival in a half-day program at our school. Her first teacher, Miss Nettie, had been Mary Pat's, too. And we were fortunate to find a deaf family to babysit for her in the afternoons.

Marcy received her first hearing aids two weeks after her arrival. Within weeks she went from a child who mimicked our speech with voiceless sounds, to a child who flapped her arms, to a child full of gestures and single signs. She was enrolled in a good school program with consistency in behavior strategies used at school and at home. We marveled that Norina Hatcher, the speech and language pathologist, was able to encourage her to produce sound when she signed and we began the process for a cochlear implant. Marcy was implanted in May; hooked up in June.

We set up a very strict behavioral management program for our new daughter. If she were non-compliant, she was sent to her room. For the first several days, Marcy would do little that was asked of her and she was marched up to her room continuously. Then we would hold or tie the door closed while she screamed and pounded the floor. It was unnerving how long she could carry on.

Within a week, Marcy was being timed-out perhaps once a day. She stopped sucking her thumb, gesturing her desires, and occasionally interacted positively with Mary Pat in play. Often, however, I would come home from a long day at work, only to have to deal with her refusal to share, sleeplessness, and screaming. Week after week, she brought the worst out in us all. And we felt we could tell no one.

Gradually Marcy learned more vocabulary and her attitude and behavior slowly began to improve. She began to be receptive of hugs and kisses. By the end of the summer, she had a 2 1/2-3 year-old language level and enjoyed conversing. We'd laugh as she'd sign and gesture long turns, only about a third of which was comprehensible. Over the summer she learned to ride a trike, jump, hop on one foot, cut, paint, and play cooperatively. She was hard to distinguish from any other four year-old in a group of youngsters!

Some members of our family had never acknowledged the adoption of Mary Pat and likewise ignored Marcy's arrival into our family. Although this hurt us, we only discussed it with a few close friends. We had a strong marriage, a strong family, and a strong community of understanding friends. It got us through the initially difficult times. Other family and friends were wonderful: showering Marcy with gifts of clothes and toys that she had never owned, and making us feel the specialness of this new child in our family.

The Older Siblings

Much of the tension and stress that exists in families with children with special needs has been alleviated in our family by the participation of our older hearing children. I remember well one night standing at the kitchen sink washing dishes shortly after Mary Pat had come to live with us. I listened to hearing aids whistle until I felt like screaming, wondering how we could carry out Mary Pat's clinical speech and auditory training goals at home and wondering if she would learn English and American Sign Language. Gradually those thoughts were interrupted by the sounds of our older girls, Breeze and Hannah, playing with their new sister in the living room. At that time they were five and nine years old. I realized from the deliberate pauses in their speech that they were carefully signing each word that they communicated with her. I heard them try to incorporate Mary Pat's speech and audition lessons into their play as we had discussed earlier that day and I realized that they were comrades in our struggle to facilitate Mary Pat's complete development. As her siblings, they shared the responsibility of raising a deaf child.

The older girls were wonderful "big sisters" to the little ones. I, myself, have never had much patience when it comes to children's board or computer games, but it's no problem for the older girls to do so again and again. Playing with their older sisters, Mary Pat and Marcy learned game rules, counting skills, and thinking strategies.

We learned quickly that Mary Pat's sisters could often get her engaged in difficult tasks longer than we could. She, and now Marcy, idolized them and the younger girls worked hard to impress them or to be allowed to play with them and their friends. The older girls provide natural reinforcement for learning new ideas. Our younger daughters were more likely to try harder or stay on tasks longer if it seemed important to their older sisters. We have contests to see who could teach which daughter new vocabulary words or new English idioms first. Each of us discovered the joy of seeing a child do something that you know was learned from you!

Our hearing children have also been imparters of much deaf awareness to other hearing children. We hear them talking with friends about adoption, deafness, assistive equipment, relay systems and the like. Somehow the girls are able to explain how a TDD works or why batteries need to be changed in a way that satisfies their friends' curiosity. They have been providing sign instruction to peers, parents, grandparents, and neighbors since Mary Pat's arrival. That experience has created a supportive community of interested learners who make them feel needed, competent and talented.

In Junior High Breeze had her own deaf friends who were integrated into her school from the Kansas School for the Deaf. They ate lunch together, saw each other on weekends, and engaged in long, very long, TDD calls. Breeze was proud of these friendships and looked forward to spending time in the dorms when we visited at KSD.

There was a lot going on in our family. We set a standard that we needed to help each other through the busy days. Sometimes we asked the older girls to check the batteries in Marcy's cochlear implant, help the little ones dress or undress, monitor a bath, or get the girls safely across the street. They read and signed stories to Marcy and Mary Pat, helped with Mary Pat's homework, fixed hair and were useful in a thousand other ways.

To me, it was a matter of teamwork. I'd say to them, "Hey, I'll make your lunch if you help Mary Pat get her "show and tell" ready for school." Hannah and Breeze seemed willing to do these small but important jobs because we attached value to them. We gave them lots of credit for their assistance and we let grandparents, teachers, and peers know how well the older girls assume such responsibility.

We also tried to reward the responsibility that our older hearing girls demonstrate for their younger deaf sisters. Their willingness to care for their sisters occasionally gave us a feeling of freedom and spontaneity that we hadn't been able to enjoy for a long time. We helped the older girls set goals for spending their money wisely and we drove them to evening choir or play practice or ran an occasional errand for them in exchange for a little time of our own. We made special events out of inviting friends over, having special desserts, rewarding them with books or treasures that they were particularly interested in to express in a tangible way that we were thankful for their attitude as members of our family. Breeze and Hannah had a rich, full life, but they clearly shared their parents' resources of time and money with their younger sisters.

Fall, 1992

In the 1992 school year Breeze was in ninth grade, involved in orchestra (first chair violin), choir, basketball, and the fall play. She was an A student and well-liked by her teachers and friends. Her life was made considerably easier that fall by our decision to exchange room and board for childcare with a deaf college student. Lori lived with us throughout the week and was off having fun or visiting her family in Missouri on the weekends.

Hannah was in fourth grade -- but sixth grade orchestra. She was also an excellent student and read endlessly. She had two deaf students in her room and thought it was nothing special that she could sign easily with them. "Mom," she claimed, "everyone can talk to them; everyone signs." Hannah had had a special love for Marcy since they became sisters and they would spend hours together, sitting on the couch, snuggling and talking. Hannah, Mary Pat, and Marcy spent the long fall weekends playing "family."

Mary Pat was six and in first grade. She was one of 12 students in her class and had a full-time interpreter. Her speech was largely intelligible except that she lost her four front teeth that year! She could now talk for herself on the telephone, order in restaurants, and converse eaily with her hearing peers. The dream we had in Illinois had come true. She was a top student; excellent reader. We still were a little worried about her ability to make friends--real friends--friends to giggle between worksheets with you and whisper to you at learning stations. Her general education teacher could sign whole sentences to her, and her interpreter often changed her role to teach a small group, read a story, or teach sign to the class. This was because we had asked that Mary Pat receive more simultaneous (rather than interpreted) communication. We wanted her to have a lot of opportunity to use the hearing her implant now afforded her. She still saw a teacher of the deaf both individually and with a small group of hearing peers each day. On Thursdays she rode the bus to KSD, played with her deaf friends, and ate dinner.

Marcy was almost five, soon to celebrate her first birthday with us. We invited all the deaf and hearing children in her classes--both public school and KSD. We felt like a celebration was due! Marcy's behavior now paralleled the other children in her class, she initiated conversations using 3-4 word sentences, and was making consistent progress with speech and audition. Marcy was a good hugger and a talented artist. And she was growing like a weed! Marcy figured out how Halloween worked after visitng three houses and loved the warmth of our Thanksgiving feast. Unlike the generation of deaf adults who preceded them, our little girls had access to the family conversation that surrounded them at these holiday meals and elsewhere. On September 17, 1992, Marcy gave me her first unsolicited kiss as I dropped her off for school!

Kent still worked as a technology resource specialist for the Kansas City, Missouri School District. He felt very appreciated in his challenging role as both teacher and facilitator, and was again working on a masters degree, taking one or two courses each semester. Graduation was in sight. His schedule required him to begin at 7:30 AM but he was home after school to meet the girls on the days he didn't have meetings or errands.

My career was at its height. The textbook I had co-authored had received strong reviews, I was administering a stimulating rural training grant, there were ample qualified graduate students applying and enrolling in the KU Deaf Education program, and I was being asked to consult throughout the country several times a year. I was a tenured, full professor--but only saw my family about two hours; on the night I taught, I didn't see them at all. Breeze made the ninth grade basketball team and I had missed all but one of her games. I continued to feel as if my professional and parenting roles were unbalanced.

Support Systems

When I think about summarizing the supports on which we have depended in the eight years that we have been raising deaf children, I can categorize them into four different groups. First, and most importantly, there are the supports within each of us as individuals. Our love for our children, our need to search and find new ways to meet their needs and our needs, our need to be responsible siblings and adults within our family are ways that we support the challenges of raising each of our unique children.

We have found that accepting both hearing and deaf people in our lives has expanded our acceptance of people of color, gay people, people from different cultural backgrounds-- and in general realizing that in diversity is strength.

Finding our inner capacity to meet the challenges presented to us each day has been a gratifying as well as frustrating experience. Utilizing the gifts of life, despite the presence of pain, and facing sorrow and unhappiness has expanded our growth as human beings. We have taken time to learn stress management and time management strategies. We have set goals for ourselves as parents and siblings, and checked our progress. We have asked for help, we have sought respite care, and we have kept our sense of humor. We continue to try to be flexible in changing our beliefs and attitudes.

Secondly, we have also found support in others. We search for safe environments to express our feelings. We talk in trust with others. Some people, fortunately, give us empathetic and objective feedback. We have found a sense of community with others who have had similar experiences to ours both with deafness and with adoption. We seek information about communication needs and knowledge and discussion of options from others. We have been the initiators of meetings if necessary, and attended conferences and meetings that others have provided. We subscribe to newspapers and journals that are relevant to our needs, are thankful to those who have been helpful, and acknowledge contributions to our lives.

Thirdly, we have found support in the differently-abled people in our community. We have supported and recognized the achievements of those who face special challenges in their lives. Dealing with negative feelings and attitudes has helped us know all people more sincerely. We have sought companionship as well as advice from deaf adults and helped facilitate others to find their inner strength.

Lastly, we have found support in ourselves as parents of deaf children. Kent and I have created time in our schedules to walk and talk about our feelings, expectations and needs. We have discovered resolutions through mutual respect in hours of conversations. We have learned to trust ourselves and our solutions. We have divided responsibilities equally and we have utilized siblings, relatives, and friends to support us in our times of need. Our relationship, our marriage, our friendship, has become stronger with the gifts that our deaf children have given us.

The Women's Music Festival

Breeze drove with me in May, 1992, to the National Women's Music Festival in Bloomington, Indiana. Renewing my interests in women's issues symbolized that my life wasn't continually focused on deafness. The festival activities were like a futurist dream: everything was totally accessible. Mary Pat was with us for the four day celebration and interpreters were provided without us even asking. Our ability to sign was valued and we enjoyed interacting with deaf women at the event. Then, in a session near the end of the conference, at a workshop about the rights of differently-abled people, a hearing woman with close ties to the Indiana School for the Deaf told me we were oppressing our girls because we were raising them using English signing. For someone that had come of age in the '70s and worked passionately for the United Farm Workers movement, I could not ignore her. For the remainder of the conference I struggled to enjoy Mary Pat as she interacted with strong deaf women, struggled to see the gift Breeze gave her as she interpreted daily in the children's program, struggled to see the strengths of our family and the strong self-confidence and skills that all the girls were developing. I knew on one level that the woman did not know of our efforts to raise bilingual/bicultural children and had stereotyped us, yet I committed myself to the writing of a paper on Deaf Culture for hearing families.

Deaf Culture For Hearing Families

Many hearing parents with children who are deaf or hard of hearing adopt a bilingual-bicultural perspective in raising their children. This means that they set goals to facilitate their children's acquisition of both English and American Sign Language and provide opportunities for their children to participate in activities sponsored by both hearing and deaf groups. The situation for these parents is similar to that of parents who are raising children born in another country, raising children who are gay, or raising children in families whose religious orientation is different from that of mainstream America. These parents, like Kent and I, recognize that they will need to provide special opportunities for their children so that their family can learn to utilize more than one language (or mode of communication) and respect more then one culture.

Many parents who are motivated to provide a bilingual-bicultural experience for their child find it difficult to do so. Problems may occur, for instance, in families with two parents working outside the home, single parent families, and families living in rural areas. I encourage families to subscribe to publications produced by deaf people, such as the *Silent News,* the *NAD Broadcaster* and the *Deaf American* (published by the National Association of the Deaf), and the annual Deaf American Monograph series on deafness and related issues.

These publications present a wide range of views on a variety of issues. They allow hearing parents to experience the "deaf perspective" on social, political, economic, and educational concerns. The articles they contain may be serious or humorous and are usually quite short. Families may subscribe individually or suggest that their parent group or local library subscribe.

Families may also benefit from membership in the National Association of the Deaf (NAD), a national organization with affiliates in most states. Membership is inexpensive, and most state groups sponsor a wide variety of activities throughout the year. The NAD also sponsors a national conference that convenes in a different location every two years. This conference offers sessions on a wide variety of topics and would be a fun and informative family event.

Parents might also consider adding their names to the mailing list of the Gallaudet University Bookstore. This assures that they will receive a new catalog of merchandise sold through the bookstore twice a year, as well as flyers and other promotional materials. Parents may want to order one special book about deafness for their child's birthday or for a particular holiday. They might set a goal of buying one book annually for their local or school library. Finally, they might encourage their local or school library also to purchase at least one book or videotape related to deafness annually.

Parents who feel they are not receiving enough information about deafness may wish to contact the teacher training program at a university or college in their state. Faculty in deaf education programs usually receive numerous newspapers, journals, and newsletter pertaining to deafness. Examples of this type of literature include *NTID Focus* (published by the National Technical Institute for the Deaf), newsletters published by schools for the deaf, and catalogs from training programs. Most of these professors and instructors would be pleased to share either the materials themselves or the addresses where they can be obtained.

Parents attempting to promote a bilingual/bicultural perspective in their families can also attempt to form genuine friendships, based on common interests, with people who are deaf or who have deaf family members. It has been our experience that such friendships blossom and are more long-lived if they are based on activities of true interest to those involved. It is difficult to go to a deaf club where one knows none of the members or to a church (even though a large number of deaf people might also attend there) where no one recognizes any one. We have been more successful inviting one or two deaf couples to birthday parties, card parties, or family dinners, or to go bowling. This allows us to establish a relationship and find topics and activities that are of mutual interest. Some of these friendships have lasted for years, others for a shorter period of time.

Hearing parents who are intrigued with the idea of inviting one or two deaf adults to a dinner party may consider a small dinner with several couples as guests: one or two deaf couples and one or two hearing couples, like themselves, with deaf or hard of hearing children. The hosts might investigate the possibility of hiring an interpreter for the occasion, so that communication does not become an issue of concern. Many hearing parents avoid contact with deaf adults because they do not feel they sign well enough to communicate; if they feel that hiring an interpreter would ease communication and allow them the experiences they desire, then doing so is not a bad plan.

Families with deaf members might also attend theater events involving deaf actors. This might mean traveling to a larger city to attend a performance of the National Theatre of the Deaf or visiting a residential school where a theater event is offered. Depending on the size of the city, art exhibits, mime performances, and other artistic events that involve deaf adults may be available for families.

Finally, parents should continue to take sign classes. If they have exceeded the level of signing offered at the school their deaf or hard of hearing child attends, they might seek additional sign classes at a community college or their state residential school. Hiring a deaf adult or teen for private tutoring may also be an option. Some family members may be at a level where they could benefit from a university or college sign course. They also may be able to attend courses in deaf studies or language and deafness at a training program for teachers of deaf students. There is more to learn in sign classes than the signs themselves, especially if the classes are taught by deaf adults, hearing people with deaf family members, or professors who have studied deaf education.

Deaf Culture at School

Administrators can make sure that families with deaf or hard of hearing children are made aware of other families with deaf or hard of hearing children attending school in the same district or cooperative. It may be helpful to supply families with younger children with the names of older deaf and hard of hearing children who are willing to serve as babysitters.

In programs with few children who are deaf or hard of hearing, administrators and teachers can advocate that deaf and hard of hearing students be placed in classrooms with other children who may be familiar with signing, for example, hearing children of deaf parents or hearing children with siblings who are deaf or hard of hearing. This helps to ensure that children who are deaf or hard of hearing will have others in their classrooms with whom they can more easily communicate.

Schools also can teach functional signing to hearing children on a daily basis. School personnel can organize an annual or semi-annual "sign-a-thon" (along the lines of a spelling bee) and encourage all grade levels and teachers to become involved. This activity is an obvious way of promoting signing in the school.

Librarians at schools with deaf and hard of hearing students can add books, newspapers, and newsletters that promote respect for and understanding of deafness. Catalogs from the Gallaudet University Press, T. J. Publishers, and other such clearing houses are rich resources of current books and videotapes for both adults and children. Librarians also can work with parent organizations in their schools to make TDDs available on loan to hearing children and teachers. These can be checked out from the library and returned in the same way as are books. Making TDDs available to all children who wish to communicate with their deaf friends increases deaf awareness at school.

Schools can celebrate Deaf Awareness Week each fall with projects on any scale. Perhaps an administrator will promise to finalize a project involving deafness that hasn't yet been completed. Perhaps teachers will introduce their classes to famous deaf adults in history. Perhaps a deaf adult from the community will be invited to talk with students about his or her own school experiences. It is not the size of the project but the respect with which it is carried out that helps us all to celebrate a successful Deaf Awareness Week.

School programs that include children who are deaf or hard of hearing might organize a "deaf advisory board." This board could include deaf adults, parents of deaf children, teachers, interpreters, and involved administrators. The board might discuss deaf culture for hearing families and hearing teachers in their school, clarify issues of concern, advocate for the needs of deaf and of deaf and hard of hearing children (including the need to socialize with each other during the school day), and so forth. Deaf adults need to see that their involvement at school is genuine and appreciated.

Deaf Adults Promoting Deaf Culture for Hearing Families

Deaf adults can help families who wish to realize a bilingual-bicultural goal by making the local chapter of the NAD or the local deaf club accessible to hearing parents and their deaf or hard of hearing children. Several times a year, these groups could sponsor activities such as story-telling, family sporting events, dinners, or theatrical activities.

I'd always hoped a Deaf adult might "adopt" our family and do things with us on a regular basis. Another version of this idea would be to encourage hearing families of deaf children to adopt older deaf adults as "grandparents." Deaf adults might establish a big brother/big sister program for deaf and hard of hearing children or organize a monthly or annual potluck with families in the community. They might assist in organizing a silent weekend for families with deaf or hard of hearing children.

Deaf adults might compile a list of other deaf adults willing to visit schools and homes to talk with children about their own lives and values. Adults included in such a resource should be available to schools and families at a variety of times. Because their contact with families may have great significance, they should undertake this activity with great thoughtfulness and appreciation for the responsibility involved.

Deaf adults might share with schools and parents their knowledge of relevant publications and videotapes, obtaining catalogs and newspapers as examples, providing mailing addresses, and discussing how the materials can be utilized.

It's not easy for a child to be deaf or hard of hearing, and for hearing parents it's not easy to raise a child who is deaf or hard of hearing. But the pitfalls, the problems, and above all, the loneliness of the situation, can be eased considerably by an atmosphere of support and understanding. When the school, the deaf community, and parents pool their interests and work together, they can help make the lives of deaf children in their community richer, happier, and more rewarding. I truly believe that.

When I gave a paper containing many of the above ideas regarding "Deaf Culture for Hearing Families" at a conference on Deaf Culture held at Gallaudet University a deaf man I knew from my community questioned my authority to present a paper on the topic of Deaf Culture. I tried to summarize my thoughts, feeling that he was expecting me to be more defensive than I was. I wanted us to be allies; not on opposing teams. I represented a lot of parents, hearing parents raising deaf children. I wanted us to work together to find ways for families to become involved with deaf adults, to feel comfortable around them, and to allow their children to socialize often and consistent with them. Many parents have told me how fearful they are of deaf adults and hoped my paper would give parents and educators lots of ideas for activities so that things could improve. In my vision, we are all extended family.

<u>Adoption Issues</u>

We have never investigated adoptive issues the way we have issues about deafness, but we felt that the more people you have in the world loving you, the better off you are. We have welcomed the conferences that enable us to bring Mary Pat to Dallas to spend a few days playing with her half-sister by birth. The girls have the same birth mother and we have been able to get them together at least once a year since our families discovered each other. Mary Pat's sister is two years younger and hearing. Both girls are beautiful children, bright, and talkative.

We have always been very open with Mary Pat--and now Marcy--about their past histories. We write letters annually to the agencies where they were adopted, providing information about their current interests and activities. When Mary Pat has had to bring pictures of her family to school for a "this is me" bulletin board, she always includes pictures of her birth mom and foster parents. Mary Pat has said proudly for years, "I have three moms: my birth mom, by foster mom, and my <u>real</u> mom!" I love that line!

When we adopted Marcy, my mother came that spring to meet her. My brother Charlie and his family and my brother, Bill, came at different times to see our new daughter, too. We felt so pleased and supported by these efforts. We were just beginning to tell people more truthful versions of what Marcy's behavior had been like in the first six months of her living with us. Now that she was acquiring language through sign and learning to trust us, we could be more flexible and loving towards her. Yet, there were still plenty of days of stubbornness and confusion and we very much needed the support of the family and friends who offered it. Sometimes my own birth family made me feel like we had just purchased a new dishwasher instead of adding a child to our family. The physical visits by family members who took the time to experience our current life off-set the hurt that many of our closest family members had not acknowledged Mary Pat, and now Marcy's arrival.

Summer 1992

Marcy bounced into summer, much healthier and happier than she had been during the winter months. She was doing regular things in a regular family. Her weekly job was to empty the waste baskets and she loved having such a responsibility. She would get mad if anyone tried to interfere as she went back and forth up the stairs. The little girl who couldn't hop and could barely make it up on to our kitchen stools when she first arrived, was now able to skip, swing wildly in the back yard, sit attentively while her sisters read to her, help make cookies, and enjoy picnicking with her family. By Father's Day that year, Marcy still used no voice, despite her implant, but we worked as a family on her language development. We taped weekly goals on our refrigerator and set up tutoring times at which she "played" with her siblings using educational games.

I was worried about Marcy's progress with expressive grammar. She seemed to have plateaued and I made several video tapes of her skills and discussed them with professionals. No one could give me much advice and I fell back on a combination of instinct and tips from the available literature.

Marcy could usually make herself understood; my concern was with the structure--the form--of her comments and questions. We tried to always provide her with a correct model and, as I mentioned previously, often asked her to imitate it. I also encouraged Kent and Breeze (as well as reminding myself) to expand or recast what she signed.

In using expansions of the child's sentence or a simple recast, the adult changes just one or two major components or expands an incomplete sentence produced by the child without reordering any elements of the child's sentence.

Child: *Boat go.*
Adult: *Yes, the boat is going.*

Research has demonstrated that recasting is a powerful conversational means for enhancing a young child's attention to and analysis of to-be-acquired syntactic structures.

Recasting the utterances of deaf children can allow adults opportunities to model authentic English.

Child: *I will not be cold.*
Adult: *No, you won't be cold.*

I also tried to paraphrase what Marcy signed to assist both her acquisition of form and meaning.

"Hot spots" of acquisition (indicated in bold type in the example below) occur when children have been gathering information about form or word-meaning, are supplied needed information at exactly the right time, and use a newly acquired word or phrase.

Child: *I like to eat onions that are not cooked.*
Mom: *Oh, you like uncooked onions?*
Child: *Yeah, I like the **uncooked**.*
Mom: *Wow, I don't like raw onions!*
Child: *Well, I like them **raw**. I do.*

Sometimes I would include a simple definition of a new term in my model. For example, I might have said:

Do you want to go to the dry cleaners with me?
I need to pick up our clean clothes.
The people at the cleaners have cleaned them.
Want to go to the dry cleaners with me?

To help Marcy acquire specific vocabulary of figurative expressions, I often contrasted them with known vocabulary. For example:

Marcy, I need you out of the tub--now.
Shake a leg; I want you to get out quickly.
Please hurry--shake a leg.

Family Reunion

We had a big family reunion in the summer of 1992 and many of my relatives were able to meet the little girls for the first time. I remember feeling so relieved when my Dad met Marcy. I was worried that he would ignore her hugs and kisses as she went running up to him signing "GRANDFATHER, GRANDFATHER." After all, they had never met and yet he was the only grandpa she was ever going to have. On this special day, he laughed and hugged Marcy back. It was a significant event for me. My Dad had been adopted at four years of age just as Marcy. Marcy's lack of comprehensible speech and my father's own hearing loss (obtained while around noisy planes in the Navy during World War II) prevented the two from the kinds of interactions that grandparents usually have with their grandchildren. Even Mary Pat's speech was difficult for my Dad to understand. My father continues to only see the children once or twice a year, but he always laughs softly as they hug, Mary Pat calls him "Grampie." I'm pretty sure he likes it!

My Mom understands all the love and time that has gone into the accomplishment of what probably seems insignificant in most other families. She has a knack for communicating with the girls. She and Kent's mom, Grandma Rita, are naturals at knowing to bend down at eye level, pointing and gesturing as they talk in simple sentences.

They both took sign classes initially, but I think we sabotaged their attempts to formally communicate in sign by being so rapid and efficient at it in their presence. Had I to do over again, I wouldn't have jumped in and interpreted for them when they were trying out their signs, but just let them experiment and find their own way.

Fall found us camping with friends in Wisconsin, some of whose children were learning to sign in their own schools, and then back in school. I still tutored Marcy at home several times a week, especially concentrating on her audition and speech skills, but basically, we were just a typical, active family with girls in numerous activities, Thanksgiving with Grandma Rita, Marcy's birthday, and preparations for Christmas. Then the bottom dropped right out of our world.

A few weeks before Santa's arrival, Kent hit a train with our van as he returned home from a college exam. Breaking the news to the girls was difficult. My sign was awkward as I tried to pick my information carefully, each word packed with emotion, and my body tired from a night in the emergency room. He had broken his hip, his elbow, his nose, and a rib, and was covered with cuts and bruises. Our van and our holiday plans had been demolished. I realized as I struggled through the next few days, that I found the greatest relief among people who signed. My colleague, Lynn Hayes, whom I had called that first night when I had to go to the hospital (she claimed she had a lot of papers to grade and didn't mind coming over at all...) was a certified interpreter as well as a teacher of the deaf herself. Her ability to help me explain and expand explanations the morning after the accident proved her to be a perfect friend. And although I didn't fully realize it until later, the teachers of my children were an extremely close support. They were the family we did not have in Kansas. They were able to talk with the kids at school while I was busy with Kent's surgeries, the car, insurance, and so forth. I also hired one of my graduate students (who signed) to be with the children after school. Clear lines of communication and opportunities for intensive conversations was sorely needed at this time of anxiety and sadness.

Kent was in the hospital for three weeks, spending Christmas there. I shipped the kids off to relatives in Florida and tried to catch up at work. In early January, Kent was brought home by ambulance. My brother, Bill, arrived to help care for him, and the girls returned. Kent was in a hospital bed parked in the living room for about six weeks, unable to sign because of nerve damage to one hand and a broken elbow on the other side. Bill fed and entertained Kent, cooked meals, and taught the girls to eat bagels and cream cheese. I fell apart emotionally, took medication for depression, and, as usual, tried to pretend at work that everything was fine.

Consulting in deaf education never looked so good as it did that spring. I braved below zero weather in South Dakota, lost my hotel room to the FBI in Waco, Texas (due to David Koresh), and got caught in blizzards in Massachusetts and Kentucky. Yet, I relished hotel rooms without little girls jumping on my bed and put my energies into my inservice work. I cherished the friendships of the colleagues I had made around the country who seemed so interested in the information I was offering and so caring about Kent. I reread my own writings on support systems and explored many of the options that I had recommended to others.

By February Kent was using a wheelchair and then a walker. I took the girls to Indianapolis for their annual evaluation. Both were performing well and it was uplifting to have the staff there so reinforcing of our efforts at home. Marcy had had her cochlear implant for eight months and tested solidly as well as other deaf children who had been using theirs (and who, unlike Marcy, had worn hearing aids and had had speech therapy before the surgery). She could identify lots of environmental sounds, distinguish one syllable words from three syllables, and talked in sentences. Some words are very intelligible (no, mama, Mary Pat), but most were not. Her English language improvement and behavioral changes were a thrill to the whole team. How important professionals are to parents!

We were also able to see Vara, the little girl who had come from Bulgaria with Marcy. It pained me a bit to see how quickly her English had developed. She had no accent and didn't evidence the grammatical difficulties that Marcy did. Yet, the health and happiness of both girls was a delight to us all.

Planning for Fall, 1993

Throughout the spring of 1993 we worked closely with our school team to create an appropriate program for Marcy the next fall. She did not have the English language base to comprehend kindergarten. Some staff wanted her in the general education class for socialization, but that was not one of her areas of need as identified by the assessments that had been conducted. Rather than get into complicated discussions about the issue, we simply asked repeatedly if she had socialization needs. When team members agreed she did not, it allowed us to focus on her English language needs and her need to be kept out of general education classes.

It was eventually decided that Marcy would be placed with a teacher of the deaf for the majority of the day in the fall. She would go to the general kindergarten classroom for only about 20 minutes of free play a day and the teacher of the deaf would accompany her. Unlike Mary Pat, who was the only deaf child in her grade, there were three other children who were deaf or hard of hearing of Marcy's same age. They were going to spend half the day with Marcy and half in the general education kindergarten. I was pleased that the school would plan an individualized program for our daughter and her more self-contained placement was not something the other parents and our family discussed much. Marcy's deaf peers still spend more time in the general classroom than she does and we continue to feel that Marcy needs time with a teacher specially trained to work on English language skills and mediate her learning of subject content. Different children need different options. Luckily, our school, Scarborough, provides a range of services.

Interpreting Outside of School

The provision of interpreting services outside of school was a big concern. If the girls were involved with city or county sponsored sporting events, interpreters were provided. Often the musically-oriented events in our community were performed with interpreting without us even asking! It seemed that these groups are of a mindset that they should provide access to everyone, both physical and communicative access. Even the local movie theater gave us passes if we were seeing a show only to interpret for the girls. The difficulty came with privately sponsored activities such as softball and Girl Scouts. Our options were to interpret ourselves, pay from our family funds, or ask the private groups to pay. Horseback riding lessons were the last time I just volunteered my time. Running backward around a ring with a horse trotting down on me, was a nightmare! Sometimes we would work out a 50/50% arrangement, us paying half the expenses and the organization paying half of them. At $15-20.00 per hour, it wasn't long before we had to think twice about our daughters becoming involved in clubs and activities that other parents just took for granted. We still have not completely resolved this issue and it remains a challenging one for our family.

Friendships

Mandy, a little hearing second grader, was a special gift to our family during the 1993-1994 school year. She communicated through sign and fingerspelling easily with her classmate, and she and Mary Pat became fast friends! In fact, Mandy was Mary Pat's first REAL friend. The kind of friend that you spent lots of time with, talking on the phone (through the relay or TDD) or biking together or playing board games. Mandy abated my worst fears for MP; that she would receive a wonderful education in public school but be lonely and left out of birthday parties and "sleep overs."

Long after the girls had spent countless hours together, Mandy's mom gave me a gift as important as the gift her daughter was giving to Mary Pat. It was the gift of insight. She told me that Mary Pat and Mandy might have been friends much earlier save for her own fear. It had really only been because of Mandy's persistence that Mary Pat was eventually invited over to play. Once there, and there repeatedly, Mandy's mom, Reba, came to treasure and enjoy Mary Pat, her worries about communication and difference resolved. This part of the story, in fact, has a very happy ending. Our families became very close. We gave Mandy an old TDD when our girls got a new one for Christmas and Mandy learned to use it adeptly. Reba and Mike welcomed sign as a second language and saw its value in Mandy's life. They did all that they could to encourage the friendship between the girls, including inviting Mary Pat to spend three weeks with them in Germany, during the summer of 1995, where Mike had been transferred by the Army.

Knowing that Mandy was moving to Germany, we again asked that the children who had shown a propensity to learn to sign and lived in our neighborhood be grouped in the same class for third grade with her. In addition, the teachers wanted other hearing children who received speech services to be grouped in her room so that they could be together, and not so different, when they left the room.

There are still times when I am sure Mary Pat is not invited here or there, but there are many more times when friends are over, she's out riding her bike in the neighborhood with kids in her class, or a special friend is over playing in our tree fort. All the children at school have been taught to use the relay and can check out TDDs from the library. They do both often. As a fourth grader now, Mary Pat seems very content with her social life and is much more interested in playing with her hearing friends, from our neighborhood school, Scarborough, than her deaf peers at KSD.

Mary Pat's Self-Advocating

In November, 1993, when she was seven, Mary Pat was given an honor by Tim Rarus, a deaf adult and organizer in our community. She was invited to travel with a group of deaf adults from KSD to join about a dozen other adults to visit the governor and discuss TDD distribution in Kansas. She and I traveled by van with Tim and others to Topeka, the state capital. Tim talked to Mary Pat about the issues for a long time in the van. I was impressed with his tact; he was very politically astute and I could see the leadership skills that had been admired during Deaf President Now activities at Gallaudet. Mary Pat was interested and excited in the TDD issue and fascinated by the process. At one point when Tim asked my opinion about telephone tax being used as a funding source, I didn't understand his ASL, and Mary Pat nudged me and interpreted. It was such a role reversal that I stopped and laughed before responding to Tim.

Mary Pat was impressed by the governor's office and she was pleased to sit at a big, huge table among her deaf friends, all of whom dwarfed her. I sat in the back, out of her way. Tim waited until most of those present had discussed TDD distribution from various viewpoints with Governor Finney. Then he introduced Mary Pat, the last speaker. When it was her turn, Mary Pat stunned me by dropping her hands and speaking in the realization that the governor would not understand her sign. I had never seen her not sign in public or code-switch to oral English-only. I began to speak for her, just to make sure her message was not missed and also to make it easier for the interpreter to sign to her deaf friends. She said: "Governor Finney, I know you are a very important person, but I am missing school today to talk with you." (The Governor was putty in her hands now). "Telephones cost $30.00 or $20.00 dollars but TDDs cost about $130 dollars. Do you think that's fair?" (The governor shook her head to match Mary Pat's intensity.) "Everyone should have a TDD so they can call friends, for emergencies--and to order pizza!" (The room exploded in laughter.) "I think every deaf person in Kansas should have a TDD." And then like an advertisement on T.V., she finished: "Thank you for your time."

It was a proud moment, but I was also very relieved. I had hoped she would do this well. The governor shook her hand and as everyone left the room, we took a picture of them together. Mary Pat went back to school to tell everyone she had been lobbying in Topeka with her deaf friends. Just as proudly, she wore her "Deaf people can do anything" T-shirt when she went to KSD later in the year to talk with I. King Jordan, the deaf president of Gallaudet University.

"I can have two schools, right Mama?" she asked me one day as we drove over to KSD for a weekend event. Mary Pat seemed to be realizing that she could be a apart of both the hearing and the deaf world and that there were advantages and good feelings associated with both.

A New Implant

Mary Pat is a bilingual signer of English and ASL as well as a stellar user of her cochlear implant. Unfortunately, the latter had been failing for months and every time we were in to get it checked, she had lost the function of another electrode. When she had only 11 of the original 22 electrodes working, we decided to have the device replaced. Although I was confused about why the equipment had failed and didn't want anyone to go out of their way to inform our deaf friends, I was ready to respond to anyone who had an opinion about the surgery. Unlike our first surgery, I had now seen the advantages of the cochlear implant for Mary Pat.

Despite the fact that this was our third cochlear implant surgery in two years, we were still nervous on the morning of the surgery. We appreciated the honesty of Dr. Ator, the surgeon, who had never taken out a device, and the friendship of Sandy Keener, our audiologist, who visited us repeatedly in the waiting room throughout the morning. The implant came out easily, the new one went in completely, and a month later, Mary Pat was performing as well as she ever had. A year ago, we bought the Spectra 22 processor for each girl and have witnessed more improvements still with their abilities to speak and hear.

Marcy Learns to Read

Most parents would not be able to tell you the exact day, let alone moment, that their child learned to decode print, but I can. It was November 10th, 1994, at 8:00 and Marcy was in first grade. She and I were reading before leaving for school. The book had about one line of print on each page and contained approximately 100 words. The pictures provided ample clues, and Marcy had learned to use them to help her attempt to read such basic stories. Midway through the story, she came to the sentence "Wait a minute." Marcy looked down reluctantly at the list that had been placed by her side on the table for reference. It had been read together at least 20 times over the weeks. It said, "1. Look at the picture. 2. Read the sentence; does it make sense? 3. Sound out the word." This time, the picture did not cue the phrase. Reading the sentence for assistance and using the English grammar did not seem to help Marcy either because she didn't know the first or third words of the phrase.

I tapped Marcy's shoulder. "The picture is not helping, reading the sentence is not helping, maybe you can sound it out," I suggested. If Marcy could phonologically-decode the word, she would join the many hearing children who had become readers by using a strategy that was highly collated with proficient reading   "Can you sound it out," I asked Marcy, wondering if she had sufficient hearing from her implant to be taught this skill. Certainly neither Marcy's teachers nor her parents were going to be conveniently around for the rest of her life to simply tell her a word she wanted to decode.

Books and chapters about reading and deafness, few as they are, dodge all around the topic of exactly how a teacher might teach a deaf child to read. It had been documented that when deaf children are given the opportunity to read a story in context, many words that are indecipherable on the first attempt, might be read successfully after several independent tries. But what if the deaf child can't decode the word using the context? What other strategies are taught to these children so that they can independently read? Little work has been done that would answer this question.

If a child is not to be taught to "sound out words," to be able to break initial phonemes apart from the rest of a word (e.g., s at) and put sounds together to form words (e.g., b a t), to discriminate differences in highly similar words (e.g., run, ran) and so forth, then a sight-word approach is the general approach that remains. However, research hasn't shown this to be☐ a very efficient method.

I had integrated experiences with visual strategies as I tried to facilitate Marcy's reading in the last few weeks--and with some success. One day, for example, she had self-corrected her reading of "Moe," a name, from the word "more," as they both appeared in the same sentence. I had also fingerspelled words for which there were not signs close to my mouth, trying to pair the two strategies (fingerspelling and speech reading). I also asked her to write at least one word each day, usually one from one of the current stories, "to fluency," (independently and accurately). If she could write the words, perhaps she could learn to independently read them.

Sometimes finding words within words allowed her to figure out words she had been unable to read. For example, she found the word "no" in "snow" and knew from the picture that the word had something to do with winter. Saying "no" helped to sound out "snow;" finding "now" in the same word, did not. Marcy had to learn that finding little words within larger words was sometimes helpful; sometimes not.

At each session, after Marcy had read two or three of the books she was using with one error or less, I would give her a new book of the appropriate level. She would hold it, turn the pages, and look at the pictures. Then she would try to read it through, uninterrupted and without correction. Over time, she looked less and less at me during this part of reading together, although she would always sign and speak the words on the pages, be they right or wrong. I would not correct her, but would, instead, take notes of self-corrections, skipped, or mis-signed words.

On the third time through, I would stop Marcy at the spots where mis-signed words had occurred. For self-corrections, I would ask her why she changed her mind. At this point, she was not able to tell. I would discuss and model language for her as to how she probably looked at the picture, read the sentence for meaning clues, or even used sound (e.g., "Maybe you knew it was not beautiful, because it started with "p", right?"). I would feed her reasons, hoping that someday when I asked her, she would remember these models and have the language to discuss her insight into these strategies.

We made a book of word families, adding new words to the separate lists on each page when Marcy would read them in a story. I would cover my mouth and asked Marcy to find, for example, "pop," given a list from a page in the book that also listed "mop," "stop," and "hop." The speech and language pathologist at school worked on similar activities.

If Marcy could not read a word and the picture and syntax did not clue her, (and the mis-signed word was not a good one for the word families activity,) my recourse was to cover my mouth and say the word, often repeating it a second time in the context of the sentence, and then in isolation again. Sometimes Marcy could "hear" enough of the word that given the pictorial and grammatical context, she could guess it correctly. Other times, if she couldn't get it "audition only," I would drop my hand and allow Marcy to speechread my saying the word with voice. Sometimes she could get it this way, too, especially if I spoke it within the short sentence of the story. But at least half the time, I eventually simply had to "give" her the word, (the sign for the word).

Once a week, I would ask Marcy to sound out a specific set of words (e.g., moon, soon, sat, mat, pat, pet, met, etc.), and chart whether she signed each word without correctly pronouncing it, sounded it out, but wasn't able to show her comprehension by signing it, or do both--sound it out and sign it to me. With this "cloze" set of words, Marcy slowly began to be able to sound out highly similar words and sign them. Five weeks into the program, on the morning documented here, she applied the technique to an unknown word in one of her stories.

Unlike many deaf children Marcy brought many beneficial skills to the task of reading stories. She lived in an affluent family, with two college-educated parents and three older sisters, and saw reading done and valued by them all. Various reading materials were plentiful in her home (e.g., adult and children's magazines, worksheets, at least 500 children's books, etc.) and family members regularly worked on one of three computers. She went to the library at school and with her parents, and she spent time daily at her own writing table, filled with art supplies, pens and markers, and lots of paper. All her videotapes and software discs were labeled with both icons and print, and many of her possessions were labeled (e.g., two of the drawers in her dresser had cards with printed letters "play clothes" taped on them so she could be independent in changing her clothes after school). Two spots in the house, one of which was in her bedroom, were designated as children's reading areas with books that could be easily reached and comfortable pillows close at hand. Her parents or her sisters read her stories, or she watched signed versions on videotape of about 20 tales (although these were not signed in her home language). Finally, she got regular mail from her grandmothers, and "wrote" to one of them, along with her sisters, about once every two months.

Marcy had missed many typical childhood experiences, but her preschool program in the United States and the traveling that was done with her family each summer gave her a rich experiential base. There hadn't been a story that her mother and she had read together during the fall of her first grade year for which she was unfamiliar with the context (e.g., farm, baseball game, ocean, mountains, etc.).

We also believed that another strength Marcy brought to reading was her attempt to sign every word on the page of the book that she was reading. One day, for example, she came to a sentence, "They ate the rest of the bread." She signed eight signs for this sentence, one for each word plus a past tense marker to make the sign for "eat" into "ate." Some adults and children might not sign the phrase "rest of the bread" with a sign for each word as she did, but use of this type of signing by those at school and home gave her a direct speech and expressive sign match with the printed word. Those using the system that Marcy used, Signing Exact English (Gustason, Pftezing, and Zawolkow, 1973), would also sign words with multiple meanings with the same sign (e.g., the word "run" signed in the same way no matter if the meaning differed) and sign figurative expressions literally (e.g., an expression such as "hold your horses" signed with four signs, one for "hold," one for "your," one for "horse," and one for the plural "s").

Another advantage that Marcy and I had over many other parents or teachers reading with their deaf children or students was that Marcy's early reading abilities had been assessed on a package of tools and she was placed into a level for reading that was only slightly above her independent level (along the lines of the Reading Recovery Program). I chose predictable story books for her from a set that had been "leveled" and were available at public and school libraries. Five weeks earlier, when we had started reading together, Marcy was using Level 4 books; on the morning she broke the code, she had progressed to Level 9.

On November 10, Marcy came to the sentence, "Wait a minute." She had independently tried the two strategies listed on the sheet of paper beside her, and looking at me with a resigned expression, lowered her head to attempt to sound out the word. "WWWWWW.....aaaaaaaa........tttttt," she said. I sat and waited, a look of fake encouragement on my face. Then, the wheels turning, she shouted at me, "Wait! It says 'wait'."

Marcy smiled broadly, and then added, "I figure it out. I did it myself." After hugs all around, with claps and praise abounding, she settled back down and, using the newly read word, the syntax of the phrase, she read the word "minute" by sounding it out. It came so fast this time. She continued to the next sentence, but I tapped her and looked apologetic. "We have to stop," I signed, "school." We ran to make her lunch and get her out the door, promising to read together again that night. A week later she asked for a reading lamp by her bed.

Five weeks later, Marcy attempted to sound out almost every unknown word. She was working to understand that not all words are so easily decoded (e.g., "thought," "night") and I was trying different ways of intervention when Marcy correctly pronounced a word but did not know what it meant. It was a delight to watch her carefully, phonemically decode a word, think, and then sign the word with a laugh of success. Four months into the program, she was reading level 15 books and unsolicited comments from the general education first grade teacher about her reading ability were very positive. By the end of the school year her English language abilities were assessed to being approximately the 4-5 year range when compared to hearing peers and her reading at the 1.5 grade level on a standardized reading test.   She had lived in America for a little more than three years!

1994-1995

Marcy completed first grade and is now in second. She has the advantage of having both a general classroom teacher and her teacher of the deaf.   She loves school, has lots of friends, and just learned to ride a bike. Her English language is still about two years delayed and her speech is becoming clearer but about half of what she says is unintelligible. We have no way to formally assess her ASL abilities, but she can communicate with any deaf person she meets.   Marcy has tested "average" on the curriculum probes that are conducted and brings home A's and B's on her report card (compared to hearing peers). I go from great moments of worry to whole weeks of placid trust in her school staff. She is a smart girl but she missed a lot of important years sitting in that Bulgarian orphanage.

Mary Pat is still a top reader and her report card is evidence of academic success. Everyone finds her a delight. She still uses an interpreter receptively in the general classroom, but speaks for herself when called upon. She and her peers no longer sign during informal conversations. Mary Pat wants to be a model (thank you, Heather Whitestone), is very adept at gymnastics, and is seemingly comfortable with both hearing and deaf friends. We still have her go to KSD one day after school to keep up on her ASL skills and be with older deaf children and adults. Most days, she and Marcy play well together and clearly, Mary Pat is Marcy's biggest asset.

She explains everything to her little sister, using a variety of communicative means. When Mary Pat flew to Europe this summer, she became bored on the long airplane ride and wrote the following letter to American Airlines en route: "Hello. My name is Mary Pat. I am nine years old and deaf. There is a law called ADA and the movies on the airplane should be captioned. Could you do that in the future? If you would like to reply, please print."

Hannah is in 7th grade. She is accomplished academically, in sports, and was accepted to the Olathe Youth Simphony. She has a deaf classmate, Tara, who is also on her basketball team. Tara, reports her parents, are delighted that Kent can sign directly to her. Even so, her mother and I sit on the bleachers and discuss our worries about social life and deafness. It pains me to accept that Hannah seems to need a break from deafness. She has many moments of kindness and concern, but more often she wants to talk with her friends on the phone, shop at the mall, or watch endless television. "She's a typical teen," her teacher tells me.

Breeze at 17, is president of the National Honor Society and concert mistress at Olathe South High School. She spiked her hair for two years, but grew it out to please me. She has interpreted for Mary Pat's private gymnastics lessons and for Marcy's softball, but she, too, has largely taken a break from deafness. Yet, Breeze is a fighter in her own right for equality and she cheers me on whether I editorialize about the failure of the Girl Scouts to provide interpreting or am struggling with a chapter for the Hannie book, a children's novel about being the hearing sibling in a family with deaf children. She also accompanied Mary Pat through Europe, interpreting at Anne Frank's attic, the Berlin Wall, and at the concentration camp in Dachau. The girls were so well-behaved at the Phipps' household that they were invited back to "do Italy" next summer!

Kent, Coordinator of Technology at an inner city middle school, just finished the masters degree in technology he started at three universities. I took him to Hawaii as a graduation gift because he would always have to leave his credits behind when my job would move us to another state. Recently he has been presenting to educators and parents of deaf children regarding technology and helps me to evaluate specific multimedia software with regard to auditory training possibilities. Kent serves on our school deafness advisory board and makes his share of telephone calls when an issue arises. We still spend many an early morning walking and strategizing together.

Life in the Luetke-Stahlman home is rich, and positive, and perhaps even typical! It is still my fondest hope that each of my daughters will tell me as adults that they had a good and happy childhood and that they were raised well. I expect them all to be self-supporting and to make a contribution to society. And I fully believe that Mary Pat and Marcy will become bilingual-bicultural adults, able to advocate for themselves and others, and that they will be the best of friends. Personally, I know my life is richer for having lived so intimately with each member of my family.

98

OTHER PRODUCTS from MODERN SIGNS PRESS, INC.

Basic Tools and Techniques
Teaching and Learning Signing Exact English
Student Workbook
Video Tapes
Curriculum Tapes
Beginning level – 14 lessons
Rather Strange Stories (Intermediate level)
Visual Tales (available in Signed English or ASL)
The Father, The Son and The Donkey
Village Stew
The Greedy Cat
The Magic Pot
The House That Jack Built
Signed Cartoons (available in Signed English or ASL)
Three Pigs, Three Bears, Casper, Popeye, Raggedy
Ann, Superman, Rudolph, Elmer & Bugs,Daffy
Duck, Bugs Bunny, Felix the Cat, Cinderella
Animal Antics
Shipshape Shapes
Numbers
Show and Tell Stories
Series 1 – Brown Bear, Brown Bear; and, This Is Me
Informational Tapes
Deafness the Hidden Handicap
Growing Up with SEE
Children's Collection
Coloring Books
ABC's of Fingerspelling
Sign Numbers
Storybooks
Talking Finger Series - Popsicles are Cold, I Was
So Mad, Grandma's House, Little Green Monsters.
Jean's Christmas Stocking
In Our House
Be Happy Not Sad (includes coloring workbook)
Grandfather Moose (finger rhymes)
Cosmo Gets An Ear

Greeting Cards
    Color Your Own Cards (in both signs and words)
        All Occasion
        Birthday
        Christmas
Special Products
    Music In Motion
    Pledge of Allegiance Poster
    Signing Exact English in Spanish
    Sport Signs
        General Vocabulary
        Football
        Basketball
        Baseball/Softball
        Track and Field
        Volleyball
    Signs Everywhere
    Signing English: Exact Or Not? (a collection of articles)
    Interactive Sign Language (Software for Mac or Win.)
    Signing Bears "Cookie" and "Honey"
More Yet To Come
    CD Rom version of Signing Exact English
    More signed storybooks
Other Books by Barbara Luetke-Stahlman
    Effectively Educating Students with Hearing Impairments
    Hannie

FOR MORE INFORMATION on other products
MAIL - PHONE - FAX
TO REQUEST A FREE CATALOG

Modern Signs Press, Inc.
P.O. Box 1181
Los Alamitos, CA   90720

310/596-8548 V
310/493-4168 V/TDD
310/795-6614 FAX

Mary Pat, 3 yrs. old with Barbara 3/93

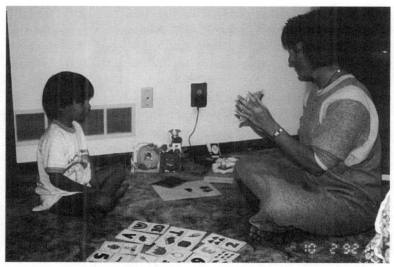

Audition training with Marcy (4 yrs. old)
Approximately 6 months after adoption. 10/92

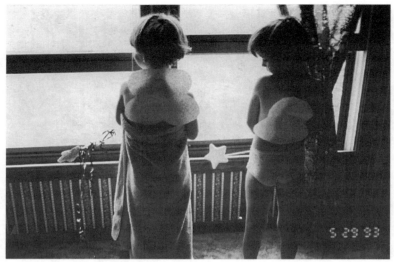

My little angels   5-93
Mary Pat - 7yrs. old, Marcy - 5yrs, old.

2nd grade 5/94
Mary Pat with our dogs for show-n-tell

Family vacation at Pikes Peak 7/94

" Best friends "
Mary Pat (8yrs. old) and Mandy

Grandma Bette and Mary Pat (8 yrs. old) 6/94

Summer 1995
Diane interpeting for Mary Pats softball

Grandma Rita and Mary Pat (8 yrs. old) 11/94

Family portrait